Near Battens
East Wharf

HAMPTON
STYLE

HAMPTON
STYLE
HOUSES ■ GARDENS ■ ARTISTS

BY
JOHN ESTEN
WITH
ROSE BENNETT GILBERT

PHOTOGRAPHS
BY
SUSAN WOOD

LITTLE, BROWN AND COMPANY
BOSTON·TORONTO·LONDON

ENDPAPERS:
Pages from Thomas Moran's East Hampton sketchbook, 1880.
Front: "Near Bathing Place." Back: "The Pond" (Hook Pond).
Courtesy East Hampton Library.
FRONTISPIECE:
The Wainscott windmill, built in Southampton
in 1813 and moved to Wainscott in 1942.
HALF-TITLE:
Clara Wells Lathrop, *Amagansett, Long Island,* 1892.
Watercolor, 8 × 14¾. Collection of James Shields, Jr.
The windmill was moved to Amagansett from Setauket in 1829.
PAGE VI:
A sculptured weather vane made by artist Balcomb Greene.

FIRST EDITION

Library of Congress Cataloging-in-Publication Data

Esten, John.
  Hampton style: houses, gardens, artists/by John Esten, with
Rose Bennett Gilbert: photographs by Susan Wood. — 1st ed.
    p.   cm.
  Includes bibliographical references and index.
  ISBN 0-316-24989-0
  1. Architecture, Domestic — New York (State) — Hamptons.
2. Gardens — New   York   (State) — Hamptons.   3. Hamptons
(N.Y.) — Social life and customs.   I. Gilbert, Rose Bennett.
II. Wood, Susan. III. Title.
NA7235.N72H353   1993
728'.37'0974725 — dc20   92-40505

10 9 8 7 6 5 4 3 2 1

IMAGO

Design by John Esten
Published simultaneously in Canada
by Little, Brown & Company (Canada) Limited

PRINTED IN HONG KONG AND BOUND IN CHINA

THIS BOOK IS PUBLISHED
IN CONJUNCTION WITH THE EXHIBITION "HAMPTON STYLE,"
ORGANIZED BY THE GUILD HALL MUSEUM, EAST HAMPTON, NEW YORK.

CONTENTS

PREFACE

Try to recall the first time you saw the sea. I can, and I remember how disappointed I was at my first glimpse. I must have had in mind reproductions of watercolors or photographs of cobalt waves breaking on palm-edged beaches strewn with colored shells. The sea I first saw was leaden gray, stretching away to an unrelieved horizon. The place: Atlantic City (need I elaborate?). Later, my first summer in art school was spent in Ocean City. Better. At last I could see the beach. Then came visits to other Jersey Shore resorts, Long Beach Island and Cape May, with even nicer beaches and architecture — but no azure water, and certainly no palms.

In the mid-sixties, I was invited to spend several weeks in East Hampton — and there it was at last! The water at times is azure or cobalt; the beach, wind-scoured, wide and smooth. Then there is the landscape: as someone once said, "an artist's paradise." (But still no palm trees!)

The more than two-year preparation of this book has been an almost unmitigated pleasure. Imagine spending one's time looking at other people's houses, gardens, and pictures and never having to feel a twinge of guilt about not clocking into an office every day! However, the longer a book is in preparation, the more people there are to thank, and the greater the chance that someone may be overlooked.

Susan Wood, who photographed most of the images in the book, is a truly kinetic person. She can't take a picture without climbing a ladder, scaling a fence, or straddling someone's roof. But she always gets the picture, and by some curious quirk, the photographs seem to look serene. Her assistants know otherwise and must be praised for their interest, determination, and patience. Randy Handwerger was with us almost every day, all the way. And when she couldn't be, second assistants Eesha Williams and David Kohen filled the breach.

Rose Gilbert took on the onerous task of transforming my research and often garbled notes into this spirited text.

In conducting that research, I am particularly indebted to Ronald Pisano, who knows more about William Merritt Chase than anyone else. We have drawn generously from his scholarship on the two schools of landscape painting of Long Island.

Dorothy King, librarian of the Long Island collection of the East Hampton Library, has been generous with her knowledge, advice, and time. It was Miss King who suggested using pages from Thomas Moran's East Hampton sketchbook as endpapers for the book.

Betty Sherrill opened doors and garden gates of her Southampton friends' homes and on several occasions escorted me personally.

I am indeed grateful to the architects, interior designers, landscape architects, and many others who allowed us to photograph their homes and gardens, and who graciously endured the disruption that's always involved. I would like to thank not only these people but also the members of their staffs who were so helpful: John Christensen, *David Anthony Easton Incorporated;* Louise Cursio, Glen Lawson, and Melissa Rudt, *Mark Hampton;* Steve Wagner and Elizabeth Kennedy, *Lois Sheer and Associates;* Armand Le Garder, Patricia Burns, and Randy Correll, *Robert A. M. Stern;* and Dale Montgomery, *McMillen, Inc.*

Many other people have helped make available the works of art and vintage photographs that give this book a broader perspective: Diana Edkins of Condé Nast Publications; Averill Geus, curator of the "Home, Sweet Home" Museum; Steve Hadley of the East Hampton Historical Society; Helen Harrison, director of the Pollock-Krasner House and Study Center; Harrison Hunt, curator of history at the Nassau County Museum; Robert Keene, town historian for Southampton; Larry Landon of the American Academy of Arts and Letters; Alicia Longwell of the Parrish Art Museum; Dale Neighbors of the New-York Historical Society; Barbara Woytowicz of the New York Public Library; Nancy Halliwell and Harry McKee of the Fenn Galleries; Lawrence Di Carlo and Neil Winkel of the Fischbach Gallery; Pamela Johnstone of the Hirschl & Adler Gallery; Sidney Mickelson of the Mickelson Gallery; and Nancy Becker, Jane Benepe, Phyllis Braff, Ralph Burack, Gordon and Peggy Davis, Miki Denhof, Marjorie Dietz, Ted Dragon, Alexandra Eames, Anne Edelstein, Alice Fiske, Peggy Freudenthal, Anita Friedman, Ann Garcelon, Donald Gaynor, T. Balcomb Greene, Georgia Griffin, Eve Gromek, Rosalie Gwathmey, Robert Hefner, Anita Hoffman, Gillian Jollis, David Joseph, Lee Minatree, Ruth Mueller, David Nisinson, Carol O'Neal, Joseph Ryle, Erika and Bill Shank, Michael Solomon, David Speer, Erica Stoller, Ed Watkins, Raymond Wesnofske, Enez Whipple, and Don Zarnow, who have greatly contributed to this book in a variety of ways.

I especially want to thank Joy Gordon, director of the Guild Hall Museum in East Hampton, for enabling this book to materialize on the walls of the museum. Working with Christina Strassfield, curator of the museum, and her associate Tracey Bashkoff has been a continuous pleasure.

In other special ways, our editors, experts, and friends at Little, Brown and Company have helped make this work a reality: Ben Ratliff, Ellen Bedell, Dorothy Straight, and, in particular, Ray Roberts.

After all, I *did* find the palm trees. Not in East Hampton, but on Little Plains Road in Southampton. Look on page 183 to see them flourishing in Larry Rivers's front garden! □

John Esten

On Shelter Island, ancient trees tower over box in the Sylvester Manor garden, planted in 1652 and still owned and cared for by direct descendants of Nathaniel Sylvester.

HAMPTON STYLE

When the first visitors came to The Hamptons, there were no artists, no parties, just one long, cold "weekend" when the weather stayed miserable the entire time — a few millennia, maybe more.

We're talking about the glaciers, about one glacier at least. Scientists argue that the same Wisconsin ice sheet kept edging down and then melting back some twenty-five thousand years ago over what is now New England. The glacier came laden with the rounded pebbles, fabulously rich, loamy soil, and surprising boulders that would be the making of Long Island.

When the last ice finally melted, two moraines lay interlocked along the entire length of the island. Composed of earth and debris pushed along by the glacier, the moraines run from Brooklyn Heights on the West End of Long Island almost to the very tip of the East End. There, they fan away to form the two flukes of land that make a map version of the island resemble a great whale butting the mainland. "Fish-shape Paumanok," native son Walt Whitman called it in *Leaves of Grass,* using its Indian name.

The metaphor is apt: fish, whales, and the pursuit of them would write a major chapter in the story of this little clutch of villages on the lower "fluke," or South Fork, of Long Island: Southampton, Bridgehampton, Sag Harbor, and East Hampton, the latter comprising Wainscott, Amagansett, The Springs, and Montauk. It is a long, colorful, and important story that includes giants as well as whales — giants in America's cultural, social, and industrial life. There were also Indians, Puritans, pirates, ordinary farmers and fisherfolk who lived in rhythm with the seasons, and extraordinary talents who might have come only "in season" but who would influence the course of the arts on an international scale.

In fact, two major art movements, American Impressionism in the late nineteenth century and Abstract Expressionism in the mid-twentieth century, are inextricably intertwined with the history of The Hamptons. So is a virtual Who's Who on the cultural scene during the past century, from William Merritt Chase and Stanford White to Jackson Pollock, Willem de Kooning, Sara and Gerald Murphy, Consuelo Vanderbilt, and Jacqueline Bouvier Kennedy Onassis. The list could go on to include contemporary writers; movie, theater, and rock stars; and architects and top interior designers, who not only have homes in The Hamptons themselves but also design and decorate those of the glitterati who summer there.

Three hundred fifty years' worth of remarkable forces, coming together on this thirty-mile strip of glacier-honed landscape, have created a culture so distinctive it can easily be recognized and named: Hampton Style. Defining it is not as easy. Hampton Style is historic. Visual references still abound to its beginnings in the early 1600s as a settlement transplanted from England, via Connecticut. Yet Hampton Style also is startlingly new. Avant-garde architecture continues to rise in sharp counterpoint to The Hamptons' natural backdrops of ocean, dunes, and windswept fields.

In between the extremes come the working farmhouses, imposing manor houses, and Victorian, Shingle, and Colonial Revival houses that may be the real, old thing or may be an earlier design idea replayed in Post-Modern versions.

Indeed, in a single afternoon's drive around The Hamptons today, it is quite possible to survey the entire spectrum of architecture in America for the past three and a half centuries.

The authentically old and the leading-edge new; the naturally beautiful and the beautifully manmade; the little-known and the world-renowned — they have all contributed to the look and attitude we call Hampton Style. What Hampton Style is not, therefore, is any one, specific look. What it is, all at once, is sophisticated and simple; intellectual and easy; sun-washed and, at times, star struck; and always flavored by the ocean air and favored by a gentle climate that affords the luminous light painters love and extends the growing season to encourage the extraordinary variety of gardens that is so important to this story.

All this — yet something more — distinguishes Hampton Style. The area is unique in the literal sense of the word, and again, geography plays a definitive role.

Less than 120 miles to the west of the South Fork lies another island, Manhattan Island. It may be a mere sliver compared to all of Long Island — the largest island on the Atlantic seaboard — but Manhattan has exerted enormous influence on The Hamptons since the late 1800s. If New York City has an alter ego, it's manifested here. Bare feet may replace business suits, and the pace may slow perceptibly, but in The Hamptons of today, glacial speed is a thing of the past. The area sparkles with energy, creativity, and individuality transplanted from the city that is the world center of art, theater, dance, music, finance, and international society.

On any given summer weekend, the South Fork may hold more of the world's wittiest, wealthiest, and most creative people per acre than any other spot on earth. They come as they have for the past century or so, attracted first by the simple natural beauty of the place, then by each other, and always by a certain sense of timelessness that has been preserved here, more than a hundred miles out into the Atlantic Ocean and separated emotionally from the rest of Long Island by Shinnecock Canal. Whatever changes have come about of necessity have come with a certain gentleness. The past is always present. As much as possible, the centuries have been held in check by those who fight to preserve what they came to The Hamptons seeking in the first place.

It hasn't always been that way. The Indians and wildlife thriving in the millennia after the glacier's retreat had a hard time of it once the white man arrived to stay. Those first settlers were Puritans, led, according to history, by eight men of "intelligence, ability, energy . . . and respectability in both character and education"[1] who tried to be fair in their dealings with the Long Island Indians. There were more than a dozen tribes on Long Island when the first Europeans came. All members of the great Algonquin family, they included the Manhassets, Shinnecocks, and Montauks, the latter said to be the largest tribe east of Brooklyn in the mid-1600s. Nonetheless, the Montauks had long been oppressed by the more aggressive Pequots of Connecticut, who demanded payment of tributes in return for peace (Paumanok, the Indian name for Long Island, means "land of tribute").[2]

Caught between the warring Pequots and the English, who promised protection, the Montauks befriended the latter. In the long run, however, there could be no protection against the white man's diseases, drink, and overwhelming numbers. Before the middle of the 1700s, fewer than four hundred Indians survived on all of Long Island. What remains of the Montauk tribe today is headquartered on the Shinnecock Indian Reservation at Southampton, which, with a twist of irony, has now become an extremely valuable piece of real estate.

Crab apple trees (*Malus baccata*) redden in autumn at the entrance to the garden of David and Patricia Silver on Georgica Pond, East Hampton. Garden designed by Peter Cooper.

Short and tragic as it may have been, the Indians' impact on The Hamptons' story is indelible. Without them, the area's heritage might be Dutch rather than English. The Dutch had already settled the western end of Long Island and Nieuw Amsterdam when the English began moving from their early colonies in Massachusetts to Connecticut, at Lynn, and from there in 1640 to what is now Southampton. For many, the venture had begun around the English farming and port town of Maidstone, in Kent, an area known for its rebelliousness in matters of religion and politics and for strong ideas about the rights of individuals. In fact, when those first settlers expanded from Southampton in 1648 to found the town of East Hampton, they even named it Maidstone.

The land for that 1648 development, some thirty-one thousand acres extending from eastern Southampton to Montauk, had been purchased from the Montauk Indians, from under the very noses of the Dutch. The deal might never have come about, leaving the way open for the Dutch to prevail over the entire island, had it not been for one of the most colorful early English settlers, Lion Gardiner. No Puritan himself but said to sympathize

with their fight against the English Crown and church, the tall, red-haired and far-sighted Gardiner had come to the New World in 1635 to build a fort at Saybrook, Connecticut, just across the sound from the East End of Long Island. A soldier and an engineer then in his late thirties, Gardiner also proved to be an invaluable diplomat who managed to make friends among the Indian tribes, even those hostile to each other. More than once that friendship proved essential to the very survival of the fledgling colonies.

In 1642, the sachem (chief) of the Montauks, whose name was Wyandanch, warned Gardiner that the Narragansetts of Connecticut were planning to lead a confederation of tribes to wipe out the English settlers. Exposed, the plot never materialized. Six years later, Wyandanch again sided with the English, this time against the Dutch, who journeyed to Southampton in 1648 intent on buying East End land from the Indians. The sachem accepted Gardiner's counteroffer and sold to the English instead.

Wyandanch and Gardiner were already accustomed to doing business together. In 1639, the sachem had sold Gardiner the large island tucked

An allée of Kwanzan cherry trees in full spring dress leads to the seventeenth-century Baker house in East Hampton.

between the North and South forks that bears his name and remains in his family to this day. Predating the colony at Southampton by a year or so, Gardiners Island was actually the first English settlement in all of New York, and his daughter Elizabeth was the first English child to be born in the state.

Succeeding generations of Gardiners have continued to play important roles in the history of The Hamptons, New York State, and beyond. In the next generation on Gardiners Island came the pirates, who also color the Hamptons' story. In this case, no less a legend than Captain Kidd landed on Gardiners Island. There he buried part of the treasure he'd lifted from a ship in the Indian Ocean. That the ship belonged to the Great Mogul was the beginning of a sad ending for Kidd, who was actually an upstanding New Yorker, we're told, who lived on Wall Street, helped found Trinity Church, and commanded British privateers in the war between England and France. The Mogul's ship had been sailing under French passes, so Kidd's was an act of war, not piracy. But never mind, tangled politics got him hanged in 1701.

Another Gardiner offspring pirated away the heart of U.S. president John Tyler. Julia Gardiner, a celebrated beauty known as "The Rose of Long Island," had been a guest with her father, state senator David Gardiner, on a ceremonial cruise aboard the steam frigate *Princeton* on a fateful day in 1844. The ship's gun burst during the ceremonial firing, and the senator was among those killed. Also aboard but unharmed was the president, who comforted the distraught Miss Gardiner and saw her safely to shore. A widower thirty years her senior, President Tyler soon became the first U.S. chief executive ever to be married while in office. Of course, the first couple made occasional visits to Gardiners Island and East Hampton, which caused a stir on local streets.

Yet another island enriches the history of the East End. Lying closer than Gardiners Island in the great V the moraines left between the South and North forks, Shelter Island was included in a generous grant from England's King Charles I to Scottish poet and statesman William, Earl of Stirling, in 1637. The earl promptly appointed one James Farrett to act as his agent, and when Farrett made a tour of inspection the following year, he became the first white man to set foot on the island. Long known to the

"Rowdy Hall," when it was located on Main Street. The ca. 1750 building had already been moved once before it arrived at today's address, 111 Egypt Lane. Courtesy East Hampton Historical Society, East Hampton, New York.

Indians as Manhansack-ah-quash-awamock — "an island sheltered by islands"[3] — it would live up to its name as a haven for persecuted English and American Quakers. The island later became home to Nathaniel Sylvester, and we read that George Fox, founder of the Quakers, visited, once preaching to the Indians from the steps of the Sylvester manor house.

A member of a wealthy English family with ties to the ill-fated King Charles I, Sylvester left England when the monarch fell and came (on his wedding trip in 1652) to Shelter Island. There he built the manor house for his bride and planted the boxwood that still survives in the remnants of their original garden. (By Sylvester family tradition, the box are decorated with gold leaf when the heir of the manor brings home a new bride.)[4]

That garden is the oldest in New York State and one of the earliest existing on the entire eastern seaboard, and it would have many emulators in the centuries to come. As the original settlers put down roots, literally, they focused first on gardening for survival, learning from the Indians how to cultivate the new and sometimes strange plants they found in the New World. All the while, they carried memories of a more gracious way of life left behind in England, and at the first opportunity, they tried to re-create the kinds of gardens they remembered from home. Letters sent aboard ships bound for England were filled with requests for seeds and favorite plants, some of which (such as dandelions and timothy) took so enthusiastically to their new venue that they escaped through the garden fences and into the wild to become field weeds today.[5]

In the rich glacial soil of Long Island, almost anything would thrive. Writing in *Beautiful Gardens in America* in 1915, Louise Shelton remarked about "the marked softness in the . . . climate especially near the sea," one reason, she concluded, that Southampton of that day "in proportion to population has probably a greater number of gardens than any town in the State, almost all of them designed and developed by their owners."

Gardens in The Hamptons today — like the area's homes — are as varied as the personalities of the owners who design and develop them. In the centuries that followed its founding, the East End would turn gradually from a farming- and fishing-based community into a Great Escape for city people. Foremost among the "es-

Leon Moran, *East Hampton Cottage,* ca. 1904.
Oil on canvas, 10 x 14. Courtesy David Nisinson.
Built in 1720–1730, the house had been moved to the corner of Egypt and Hither lanes
when it was painted by Leon Moran, a brother of Thomas Moran.

capists" would be the artists, many of them New Yorkers eager to find an affordable place away from the city. The Hamptons were as affordable as they were picturesque in the mid-nineteenth century. Residents were happy enough to accept room-and-board money from the city dwellers, who began discovering the area after the Civil War. Willing even to move out of their own homes during the season, the simple folk still eyed the visitors a bit coolly. According to one oft-quoted observation of the day, "The visitors seemed like very grand people but were just furriners to us East Hampton natives."[6]

But, then, many things were indeed "furrin" to the little communities, which had such a long legacy of isolation way out on the tip of an island surrounded by ocean and bay. True, the area had once enjoyed a cosmopolitan life as a seafaring community. The port of Sag Harbor had been second only to New York City's in the days before the Revolution. But overall, life in The Hamptons remained little affected by the outside world. Many of the original — and decidedly English — names survived. So did the old Puritan virtues of hard work, morality, and independence. The earth and the sea still supported the towns as they had from the beginning. Indeed, in their remoteness, residents of The Hamptons never did feel many repercussions from the post–Civil War economic boom that stimulated the rest of the eastern seaboard.

In contrast, the Revolutionary War had had a dramatic impact. The entire island had taken a direct hit from which it had been a long time recovering. By the Revolution, the Dutch had long since given up any claim to the New Netherlands (in 1664), and the residents of The Hamptons had settled into the sometimes rocky relationship with England that eventually galled all the colonists into war. An early grievance on Long Island had been the Crown's tax on whale oil. Whaling was hard, dangerous work, and no one was eager to share the profits with the motherland. The issue was eventually solved by one of East Hampton's early, colorful residents, Samuel "Fish-Hooks" Mulford. An active member of the Provincial Assembly, he journeyed twice to London in the early eighteenth century to protest taxes, each time carefully lining his pockets with fishhooks against the city's infamous pickpockets. He also got the tax repealed, and whaling continued to thrive in The Hamptons (until the

A stream of Shasta daisies created by landscape architect Lois Sherr forms a transition between the manicured and the naturalized at the Sagaponack garden of Pam Bernstein and George Friedman. Photograph by Steve Wagner.

entire industry foundered in the 1860s). In the 1750s, Sag Harbor — then called Sagaponack — had been dedicated as a center of whaling activity, and by 1839 it had become one of the three most important whaling ports in the world, after New Bedford and Nantucket.

Meanwhile, the first battle of the American Revolution was fought — and lost, disastrously — on Long Island's Brooklyn Heights in August 1776. George Washington's army was forced to retreat, abandoning all of Long Island to British military rule for the rest of the war. The British quickly moved their fleet into Gardiners Bay, seized the port of Sag Harbor, and set up headquarters in Southampton. Among other things, they stabled horses in the Bridgehampton church and made off with local provisions and livestock. Relations between the residents and their captors were tense, to say the least, for the seven long years the British held the territory.

The next "invasion" of the East End, by the summer folk in the following century, was met with more enthusiasm — and, no doubt, with more than a little amazement that the summer visitors were willing to travel so long and hard to get there. The trip out to the tip of Long Island was tedious at best; the railroad did not arrive in East Hampton until 1895. Certainly the country people, already generations deep in the land, saw little in their familiar scenery to write home about. One notable exception was actor and diplomat John Howard Payne, who touched world sentiment in 1822 with his immortal homage to "Home, Sweet Home," the 1660 saltbox house (one of the oldest still standing in East Hampton) that he remembered from his boyhood there. Rough-shingled and indeed "ever so humble," the house and its similar neighbors along broad, grassy Main Street gave East Hampton the nostalgic appeal of a village caught in time. Windmills whirling in the distance, grazing cows and sheep, and the famous geese that dominated Town Pond also charmed the city-weary in the late nineteenth century. They went home from their holidays and told their friends.

Thus The Hamptons had already become a seasonal draw for vacationing families when the actual drawers and painters first started coming, led in 1878 by a group of good-fellow artists who called themselves The Tile Club. Gathered under that tongue-in-cheek name (it was supposedly an ironic

Celebrated illustrator Hilary Knight created a natural water garden beside his home in East Hampton, where native bulrushes, water lilies (*Nymphaea odorata*), and *Iris Pseudacorus* flourish.

response to the current enthusiasm for decorative arts over serious painting) were a number of artists who would be taken quite seriously in the annals of American art. That year Tile Club members included the likes of Winslow Homer, John Twachtman, Edwin Austin Abbey, and J. Alden Weir. Organized a year earlier — their first annual dinner had been held in Homer's New York studio — the spirited club decided to undertake a sketching trip together to East Hampton. Most likely their choice of destinations was encouraged by Homer, who had spent several weeks there in July 1874.

Drawn by Payne's reputation and the opportunity to see "Home, Sweet Home" itself, The Tile Club descended on the South Fork. The Hamptons' future as a center of artistic and social activity was written that summer of 1878 on canvas and sketching pad and, later, in *Scribner's Monthly*. Early the next year, the magazine published the exploits of this "chirpy... hilarious" group in an article titled "The Tile Club at Play." The widely read report, plus the artwork club members made celebrating unspoiled country vistas and wild, rugged seascapes, intrigued their fellow artists back in New York City.

A further inducement to visit The Hamptons was the current vogue among American art collectors for nature and genre scenes painted *en plein air* in the manner of the French Barbizon School. The American version of the Barbizon School soon flourished in East Hampton, attracted by the luminous light and unspoiled vistas and villages. They evoked the bucolic scenery of England and Europe but were much closer to home and easier to reach. More important, perhaps, the very idea of the simple country life had great nostalgic appeal for both artists and art collectors in the rapidly industrializing America of the 1870s and 1880s.

The Tile Club's enthusiasm was caught early on by landscape painter Thomas Moran and his wife, Mary Nimmo Moran. He already enjoyed a national reputation as the "artist/explorer of the American West," whose work illustrated part of William Cullen Bryant's highly popular *Picturesque America 1872–1874* (which also included a chapter on the South Fork). Mary Nimmo Moran would later become the first woman member of the New York Etching Club and the Royal Society of Painter-Etchers in London. Together, the Morans eventually bought a sheep pasture in which to build the Aesthetic movement–inspired house they always called The Studio. With friends such as Frederick Stuart Church and Samuel Colman, Jr., the Morans quickly became the nucleus of the art colony that took root in East Hampton.

Century Magazine noted in its October 1885 issue, "At East Hampton, there is a true artist colony, and perhaps the most popular of adjacent sketching grounds for New York artists. This popularity is not entirely due to its accessibility.... Here are rural nooks for the landscape painter, delightfully English in sentiment. Here are beach and sea panoramas, stormy cloud-battles, or shimmering calm for the marine painter.... Here are costumes of the last century and fascinating faces for the figure painter; and here are salt sea-breezes and sunshine for all."[7]

The sun and sea breezes were equally attractive in nearby Southampton, which, according to a *New York Times* article in August 1875, was also "full of relics of the long buried past ... teeming with associations and traditions of our young country's antiquity."[8] Although Southampton boasted an active social scene in the 1870s and 1880s and artists such as Alfred T. Bricher lived and painted there, it remained for William Merritt Chase to fire the artistic scene in earnest. He did, in 1891, by establishing the Shinnecock Hills Summer School of Art at the invitation of a wealthy summer resident who was also an amateur painter. It was the first major outdoor school of painting in the country, and for the next ten years, while Chase and his family summered over in a house designed by Stanford White, students and the fashionable crowd alike would flock to Southampton.

As the tide of Hamptons-bound artists swelled, they found themselves vying for space with other vacationers on the railroad or overnight packets from New York. Soon they were also vying for space with the local folk. Stories still abound about East Hampton farmers' complaints that they could hardly get past the artists and easels in their own barnyards to milk the cows. One East Hampton homeowner, Nathaniel Dominy VII, reputedly gave the same answer whenever an artist asked permission to paint his 1715 house: "There's been paint enough wasted on it a'ready to ha' painted it inside and out," he'd mutter. But tradition has it that he never refused.[9]

For the most part, the East Hampton townsfolk tolerated the artists and their antics with stoic good humor. Only occasionally did the Bohemian life shock these descendants of the founding Puritans. One of the most popular boardinghouses was run by Miss Annie Huntting on Main Street, right next to the Presbyterian Church. Night after night, neighbors said, "the rattle of poker chips and the pop of corks could be heard until the small hours of the morning." One Sunday it simply became too much when the young revelers put their feet on the windowsills, waved their beer mugs, and sang "their most ribald French songs to the pious churchgoers." Shocked, one of them exclaimed, "Look at Annie Huntting, she's running a Rowdy Hall!"[10]

The name stuck, even after the house was moved twice, finally to the corner of Egypt and David's lanes, where it now stands. It was renovated and rented in 1928 by newlyweds Janet and Jack Bouvier, whose daughter Jacqueline Bouvier Kennedy Onassis spent her early summers in "Rowdy Hall."

"Rowdy" was hardly the word for the social set that was by now spending its summers in The Hamptons. Genteel, upstanding, and rich, they came from quiet "old money," and the sounds they added were of dinner-dance music and tennis balls being stroked over the nets at places like the Maidstone Club, organized in East Hampton in 1891. Thomas Moran was one of the founders; other artists, such as Childe Hassam and Adele and Albert Herter, were among the elite members. Southampton's Shinnecock Club, the second golf club in the country, would be designed in 1892 by Stanford White. Other clubs, among them the Devon Yacht Club in Amagansett, and the Bath and Tennis Club and Meadow Club in Southampton, would follow as the ranks of the social set swelled.

"Innate with good breeding and good family," one New York society writer characterized East Hampton in the summer of 1891. Another wrote of the area, "You wear fancy blazers, dress a good deal, play tennis and attend hops."

The social scene may have been decorous, but celebrities could always cause a stir. Ethel Barrymore turned heads when she visited her uncle, John Drew, the actor, and everyone was star struck in 1922 when Rudolph Valentino slunk across the Napeague dunes during the filming of *The Sheik*. On the art scene, the first generation had been replaced by such notables as Hassam, Gaines Ruger Donoho, George Bellows (who painted scenes of Montauk while honeymooning there in 1910), and the Herters, who also created one of the area's most extraordinary gardens on Georgica Pond.

A second wave of artists would arrive during and after World War II. Again, the names read like a cultural blue book. Fernand Léger and Lucia Wilcox spent a season in the East Hampton guest house of Sara (Wiborg) and Gerald Murphy, of F. Scott Fitzgerald's *Tender Is the Night*. Max Ernst came with Peggy Guggenheim, and other surrealists soon followed, including André Breton and Marcel Duchamp. By the end of the war, the East End had become an international center for art that was far different from the Barbizon-style and Impressionist landscapes of half a century before. In 1945 Jackson Pollock and Lee Krasner bought a ramshackle farmhouse in The Springs for $5,000 and paid for their groceries with paintings. Elaine and Willem de Kooning soon joined them. Jim Dine, Adolph Gottlieb, Grace Hartigan, Jacques Lipchitz, Robert Motherwell, Jimmy Ernst, Jane Freilicher, Fairfield Porter, Larry Rivers, Roy Lichtenstein, Robert Gwathmey, and James Rosenquist — much of the history of contemporary art has been written in The Hamptons.

That history continues to be written, just as the waves of the Atlantic continue their determined drumming and the sun goes on shining, sometimes a hundred days more each year in the East End than in New York City. The talented and the tanned continue to feel the seasonal pull to The Hamptons and the magnetic attraction to each other, to meeting offstage, so to speak, in chinos and sneakers. Now it's Lauren Bacall you may see in the next grocery aisle; Pinchas Zukerman, Steven Spielberg, or Joseph Heller whom you may pass under the elms on Main Street; or Alan Alda you may accompany on the ferry to Shelter Island.

The players are changing; the natives and year-rounders have come to accept the city people in season, just as they accept the weather and the gradual disappearance of the potato fields, half-buried potato barns, and old-time fishermen. But the charm and style of the place continue to grow. Perhaps artist and bon vivant Gerald Murphy, who made a lifework of living well, described the East End best in a letter to his wife, Sara, who was caught under the gray war clouds of London in 1914:

"I have decided it is the most satisfactory spot in the world." ☐

BEGINNINGS

Tour The Hamptons with an inquiring eye, and the entire history of domestic architecture in America can be read in the few miles between Southampton and Montauk. It's all here, from the weather-softened saltboxes of the mid-seventeenth century to hard-edged, leading-edge contemporary houses. But you'll have to look closely. Each era that has passed over Long Island's East End in the past 350 years has added its own stratum to what has come before, slowly blurring the distinction between, say, early Colonial and Greek Revival, between the shingled "cottages" of the late nineteenth century and the shingled Post-Modern revivals of the late twentieth century.

Abrupt changes — too often, in our particularly American vocabulary, synonymous with *progress* — have been spared in The Hamptons. Successive generations have remodeled and modernized, of course, to suit their evolving concepts of modern, but only rarely have they torn down houses and begun again. More often, they have moved, lock, stock, and chimney, from one site to the next.

Often such transplantations took place by water. Sometimes teams of oxen or mules would drag houses on heavy wooden skids "right down Main Street," according to Southampton's town historian Robert Keene. "There was no plumbing to worry about, remember. The move might take several days, and the family continued to live in the house!"

Such prudent recycling came naturally to the earliest settlers. Of Puritan stock, they brought with them the regard for thrift, hard work, and common sense that still distinguishes their descendants today. Besides, those early houses were much more than mere shelters. They symbolized new beginnings, a commitment to a new life in a new world.

Coming ashore at Conscience Point in June 1640, the first "undertakers," with some thirty-five families in all, found themselves in a meadow beyond which stretched the tossing Atlantic Ocean and behind which towered an untouched forest. There was little time to stand in the middle and admire. With the growing season already well under way, planting crops took top priority. Home building had to wait. Shelter was found as quickly and easily as possible in a manner they had seen in rural England: cellars dug deep into the earth and dunes. Walled with tree trunks and lined with animal skins, these dugouts were covered over with mud- and sod-plastered tree trunks and bundles of salt hay. "Be it ever so humble," John Howard Payne of East Hampton would write 150 years later.

Within months, however, building could begin on the shingle-sided saltbox houses the settlers remembered from Massachusetts and Connecticut, whence they'd launched their expedition. This unpretentious style would go unchanged in Southampton for another century and be exported as newer settlements were founded in East Hampton and beyond. Arrayed around a broad village green shaded over with elms, these houses, each with its picket fence and dooryard garden, turned the East End into a cluster of "New England" villages unlike anyplace else on Dutch-dominated Long Island.

The oldest frame house in all of New York State, The Hollyhocks, Thomas Halsey's 1648 homestead (*opposite*), still stands on South Main Street in Southampton, stalwart testimony to the determination with which the founding fathers put down their roots. So, in fact, did the founding mothers. They planted medicinal herbs, fruit trees, and vegetable gardens — for survival, not pleasure. Phebe Halsey set out her herb garden and orchard in 1648 with seeds, bulbs, and cuttings she had brought from England. From such simple beginnings have grown the later, luxurious pleasure gardens — as well as the famed potatoes and other crops — that continue to flourish in the East End's fertile soil.

Unlike the Halsey homestead and Payne's "Home, Sweet Home," both restored and open to the public today, few early Hamptons houses have remained fixed in time. Saltboxes eventually gave way to Georgian and Federal influences as houses passed from one generation to the next and the towns' populations grew and prospered. Adaptations and renovations still go on, but today they are often in reverse, as new owners look for their home's original soul. Nothing is as it was at the beginning, but much of The Hamptons' appeal through the centuries lies in the fact that those beginnings have never been lost from sight. □

The Hollyhocks, Halsey House, Southampton, built in 1648. Photograph ca. 1965.
Courtesy Nassau County Museum Collection, Long Island Studies Institute,
Hempstead, New York.

In 1648, the gentlemanly Thomas Halsey hefted the great hand-hewn beams into place for his saltbox home, built along an Indian trail near the Atlantic. Shingled against the ocean winds and warmed by a central chimney, the house promised a haven in the New World from the threats of the Old. But new dangers awaited. Not all the Indians were as friendly as the Shinnecocks, who taught the Puritans to plant corn and fish to survive that first harsh winter. The garden Phebe Halsey planted also was a matter of life or death, supplying both table and household medicine chest. Feverfew and tansy were needed to calm fevers; snakeroot and balm to treat vermin attacks; "strewing" herbs to freshen rooms. A quick trip to the garden could staunch a wound, dull a pain, even treat an ailing horse. Phebe's garden has been restored with the house itself (Henry F. du Pont, a summer resident of Southampton and founder of Winterthur Museum, was chairman; his wife, Ruth Wales du Pont, is a descendant of Phebe Halsey). Many furnishings, including pieces in the dining room (*above*), came from other Halsey descendants. Today the house offers a step back in time to Southampton's very beginnings.

One of America's earliest, the garden at Sylvester Manor on Shelter Island has a continuous history of cultivation by the same family dating to ca. 1652. Here, traces remain of the early garden planted by Nathaniel Sylvester and his bride. Here, Quaker founder George Fox preached to the Indians. In 1892 E. N. Horsford laid out a well-known water garden here, possibly with advice from botanist Asa Gray. Cornelia Horsford, his daughter, reordered the garden in Colonial Revival style at the turn of this century. Reminders of centuries past remain in the ancient box and trees and in a stone with Indian inscriptions at the edge of the lawn near the second manor house (built in 1737).

The lower garden at Sylvester Manor, redesigned by Cornelia Horsford, a direct descendant of Nathaniel and Grissell Sylvester. Photograph by Frances Benjamin Johnston, ca. 1901.

16

The melody is simple, and the words are still appealing nearly two centuries after John Howard Payne penned "Home, Sweet Home" in 1823, in tribute to the little saltbox house he remembered from his East Hampton boyhood. When he wrote the song, Payne was already renowned in the theater abroad, often playing opposite Elizabeth Poe (Edgar Allan's mother). But it was "Home, Sweet Home" that won him immortality and attracted later generations of artists to visit the "lowly, thatched cottage" where it had stood since 1660 across from Town Pond. Painted over and over again in the years since landscape artist Lemuel Maynard Wiles made his version (*above*) in 1886, the house often comes as a pleasant surprise to visitors today, who discover that there really was a "Home, Sweet Home."

Lemuel Maynard Wiles, *Home, Sweet Home*, 1886.
Oil on canvas, 11¾ x 17¼. Courtesy Guild Hall Museum, East Hampton, New York;
gift of David Tyson Foundation.

Let European artists journey to Barbizon. In the late nineteenth century, American artists marveled at the East End of Long Island, with its centuries-old English cottages and windmills. East Hampton in particular seemed a town caught in time, the picture of an earlier, bucolic life the artists rejoiced in capturing on paper and canvas. Caught here by the modern camera instead, the old Mulford house stands next to "Home, Sweet Home" on James Lane, just as it has since 1680. One of the oldest houses on Long Island, it remained in the same family for generations, until it was acquired by the East Hampton Historical Society. Built in 1804 and moved here in 1917, the Pantigo Mill is one of eleven surviving windmills of the era that so charmed early visitors into seeing a bit of Holland in their whirling blades. For the farmers, however, windmills were necessities of life in a flat land with no falling water they could harness to grind grain and saw wood.

Childe Hassam, *Fithian Farm, East Hampton,* 1916.
Oil on canvas, 21 x 60. Courtesy Fenn Galleries, Sante Fe, New Mexico.

A photograph taken in 1923, seven years after Hassam's painting, shows the Fithian house
in its new location behind Masonic Hall. Photograph by Eugene Armbruster.
Courtesy New York Public Library Special Collections.

The unchanged vistas that first attracted artists to the South Fork were not quite as unchanging as history might have it. Given the residents' penchant for moving houses around, tracking their provenance can lead today's owners on a merry chase. Geoffrey Garrett and Jacques Peltier have dug through volumes of local history tracing the Fithian house (*above,* the master bedroom with the pegged box paneling added in the mid-eighteenth century). Today the house stands on Fithian Lane in East Hampton, but town records indicate that the old (1668–1678) farmhouse was originally built on Main Street. It was still there in 1916 when Childe Hassam painted it (red chimney, *opposite*) under a lanquid summer sun. Hassam first visited the area at the invitation of fellow artist Gaines Ruger Donoho, one of many artists who bought homes in the area. Hassam followed suit in 1919, settling into Willow Bend, built in 1722 on Egypt Lane. Meanwhile, the streetscape itself was changing. To make room for the new Masonic Hall, the Fithian house was moved, later to be renovated and expanded far beyond the rustic farmhouse preserved forever in Hassam's painting.

The Hand house (ca. 1680) is almost as colorful and well traveled as its best-known owner, Captain David Hand, who served in both the Revolution and the War of 1812, then commanded one of the whaling ships that put out from Sag Harbor's busy port in the early nineteenth century. A member of one of the earliest families on the South Fork, Hand outlived five wives and went down in history, it is said, as the inspiration for James Fenimore Cooper's Natty Bumppo of "The Leatherstocking Tales." Built in Southampton as a half-house — the other half would have been added, as the owner prospered, to the right of the front door (*above*) — the old house was moved three times without disturbing the hand-hewn, pegged beams. The current owner has garlanded them with ivy (*opposite*) over a portrait of early settler Isaac Hand that was painted before 1691 by itinerant artist Abraham Tuthill.

Framed by beams that still bear the marks of seventeenth-century axes and adzes, the kitchen of the Hand house is open to the dining room. The cheerful clutter accumulated by current owner Otto Fenn, the photographer and antiques dealer, includes a collection of coin silver spoons and a hand-shaped Victorian vase — a wry reference to the family history of the old house.

Unlike most people in East Hampton, Carolyn and James Tyson must have been looking forward to cold weather that winter of 1949. They had seen, and been charmed by, the old Charles Baker house, dating to the late seventeenth century. The house had become derelict, but the Tysons bought it, and, as soon as the ground was hard, had it rolled on logs across the frozen potato fields (*opposite, below*) to the dune near their oceanfront property. Restored by Bill Simons (against the advice of an architect who suggested razing), the house now offers reminders of that rugged early life: in the beamed keeping room (*opposite, above*), a harpoon and old sea chest. The mellow blue paneling in an upstairs bedroom (*above*) is original to the house.

Landscape gardener Lisa Stamm's Shelter Island home is velvet-carpeted outside and joyous with summer colors, front and back. Myrtle topiaries and pots of mixed annuals (*above*) set the stage for a "rock group" on a back porch. Husband Dale Booher, architect and gardener, turned an old tenant farmer's shack into a pool house (*opposite*) with overtones of chinoiserie, surrounded by lantana standards in pots and plume poppies (*Macleaya cordata*).

Like many artists in the generation before him, critic and painter Fairfield Porter (1907–1975) found an endless source of subjects for his paintings on the East End of Long Island. Porter and his poet wife, Anne Channing, moved with their five children to Southampton in 1949, and his studio was soon filled with landscapes and scenes from the area, rendered under the influence of the Abstract Expressionist movement, then in its ascendancy, but always recognizable in subject matter. Except for the location, *Grape Arbor in Southampton* (*opposite*), painted in 1957, might have been inspired by the arbor Lisa Stamm has cultivated behind her own Shelter Island home (*above*). Perennials wrapped by the dry stone wall include *Astilbe taquetti superba, Nicotiana sylvestris,* and delphinium.

Fairfield Porter, *Grape Arbor,* 1957.
Oil on canvas, 36⅛ x 36⅛. Parrish Art Museum, Southampton, New York;
gift of the estate of Fairfield Porter.

The first time they stepped past the Victorian fence and into the derelict old farm building, Maury Green recalls, "we went through the floor." He means that literally. But rotten floorboards in the late eighteenth- or early nineteenth-century house didn't stop Green and his late partner, Christopher Chodoff, the New York antiques and furniture designer. They laid new slate floors and stripped the upper level to its beams to create the soaring sitting room (*opposite*), which looks out onto a garden sculpture by East Hampton artist Arlene Wingate. Green designed the bronze table and chairs.

Found in a local junk shop, a pair of 1920s-vintage mirrored chests with Lucite pulls is set against mirrored panels by the beds in Green's Water Mill cottage. Jean-Michel Frank, the great Parisian designer of the 1930s, created the plaster heads on the chests. The walls reflected in the mirrors, like those throughout the house, are unfinished cement. "They looked so fabulous, we never let the workmen put on the finishing coat," Green recalls. In an equally spontaneous reaction, artist Jane Wilson painted the roiling sky over *Former Fields, Water Mill* (*opposite*). An Iowan transplanted thirty years ago to the East End, she records the "deep stillness, intimacy and solitude" that can still be found in the flattened landscape and "big, high skies" over The Hamptons.

Jane Wilson, *Former Fields, Water Mill,* 1992.
Oil on linen, 70 x 60. Courtesy Fischbach Gallery, New York City.

TEMPLES

Stand at the end of Long Wharf in Sag Harbor and imagine the year is 1847. A lot of history has been written in the South Fork since Southampton's founding two hundred years before. Freedom and prosperity have gradually returned after the ruinous British occupation during the Revolution. The War of 1812 has been fought — actively in Sag Harbor, where the citizens threw up gunworks against the English ships blockading their port. Local life is still built around the old occupations of farming and fishing, but the latter has taken off in a new, dangerous, and extremely lucrative direction: whaling. Sailing around the world on years-long voyages that led from the Pacific into the frozen waters of the Arctic Ocean (a Sag Harbor ship was the first to venture into a Japanese port), the whalers came home with riches and exotic souvenirs that turned the once backwater town into a thriving and cosmopolitan community. A local antiques dealer of today credits the wealth of antique Oriental rugs still found in Sag Harbor to those wide-ranging sea voyagers of the nineteenth century.

Standing on Long Wharf in 1847, you would have been lost in the raucous bustle of one of the busiest whaling ports in the world. Between 1820 and 1850, town records show, nearly five hundred ships put into Sag Harbor, filled with whale oil and whalebone valued at an estimated $15 million. The booming industry gradually grew quiet and then faded altogether as new and easier sources of oil were found in the ground and the gold rush of 1849 lured whalers to seek their fortunes in less hazardous ways. But those few decades of dizzying wealth still reverberate in the architecture and interiors of the little town more than a century later.

Turn around and imagine the extraordinary steeple of the Whalers (Presbyterian) Church, shaped like a mariner's spyglass and silhouetted against the Sag Harbor sky. Attributed to the important American architect Minard Lafever, the Egyptian Revival church (*opposite*) was built by ship's carpenters in the 1840s. Records show that they were paid just $1.50 for a twelve-hour day (the church still cost a whopping $17,000), but the workmen left their mark for posterity in the motifs that embellish the monumental, slope-sided structure. They carved blubber spades and flensing knives, tools of their whaling trade, along the roofline and organ loft.

The 135-foot steeple is gone now, a fallen victim of the hurricane of 1938, but when the church was first constructed on Union Street, it was the most imposing building in a town of imposing buildings. Sag Harbor residents poured their money into their homes and public structures. Whether they built new (the town history shows a number of devastating fires) or modernized, they did it in what was then the latest style, Greek Revival.

With its elegant classic motifs and heroic symbolism, the Greek Revival style had wide appeal in a young America that could no longer look to its earlier English sources for inspiration. Ancient forms and details — temple fronts, columns, piers, pilasters, and dentil moldings — began appearing throughout the eastern part of the country in the 1820s. The Greek Revival influence also can be found in other Hamptons towns, as we'll see, but in Sag Harbor it has survived to a remarkable degree. On second thought, perhaps it's not so remarkable, given the sudden plunge in fortunes that all but froze building activity in the town after the whaling industry collapsed in the 1870s.

Sag Harbor struggled on into the twentieth century, enjoying another, brief flurry of activity during Prohibition days in the 1920s, when bootleggers made lucrative use of the port. All these hard times had a silver lining, however: tourism. It began to gleam during the summers of even the darkest economic days when affluent visitors, many from New York City, discovered the little port and started coming to spend the season. Charmed by the town's New England overtones and by its architectural legacy, they have never stopped coming. Many such "outsiders" have rescued numerous old homes and structures that were teetering on the brink of extinction. Today a large section of Sag Harbor has been designated a historic district, ensuring that generations yet to come will be able to stand on Long Wharf and look back over a unique chapter in the history of the South Fork. □

William V. Birney, *View of Sag Harbor*, 1899.
Watercolor, 13⅝ x 9⅝. Courtesy Guild Hall Museum, East Hampton, New York.

Inspiration is abundant in Sag Harbor. Acclaimed playwright Lanford Wilson (*Talley's Folly, Fifth of July*) often works in his renovated Sag Harbor house (ca. 1845), a splendid example of the Egyptian Revival style. The chairs in the living room are French Empire, 1810. The griffin-backed chairs were made by Philadelphia cabinetmaker Joseph Barry. A juxtaposition of Sag Harbor styles was caught by William V. Birney in an 1899 watercolor (*opposite*) of the Egyptian Revival Whalers Church behind the Italianate steeple of the Methodist Church (1845). Neither steeple was replaced after the hurricane of 1938.

Wilson crafts his Broadway hits in the book-lined workroom he has added to his Sag Harbor house and hung with works from his collection of self-taught twentieth-century American artists: *Elvis* (*left, on stand*) is by Howard Finster; the cutout painting of a man is by Mary T. Smith; Minnie Evans painted *Crucifixation* ca. 1940. Outside (*top*), Wilson's all-white garden of magnolias, lilies of the valley, bleeding hearts, and dogwoods surrounds a section of a limestone fountain from Newport. A wrought-iron Victorian planter (*above*) brims with summer color.

The centuries meet around the shores of Southampton's Lake Agawam. Set into a background of gently rolling hills and dunes near the ocean — nearer still to the very heart of the modern town — the lake takes its name from the Indians. Before the Puritans changed it, probably to honor the Earl of Southampton, a leading force in the colonization of the New World, the entire area had been called Agawam. Among the elegant homes that ring the lake today is this ca. 1840 Greek Revival house (*opposite*). It turns its classic face to historic South Main Street, while its garden (*above*) sweeps in a graceful curve all the way to the water behind. Across the lake, the limestone War Memorial, built in 1923, rises in tribute to Southampton heroes of the early twentieth century.

Top: World War I Memorial. Photograph ca. 1940. Courtesy Nassau County Museum Collection, Long Island Studies Institute, Hempstead, New York.

Ornate and gracious, the Hannibal French house stands along "Captains Row" in Sag Harbor, a domestic monument to the enormous prosperity of the whaling industry. Now home to Julienne and John Scanlon, the house dates to the early 1800s but was remodeled in the 1860s by French, wealthy owner of a whaling fleet, who added the ballroom (*opposite*) and Greek Revival detailing. *Above:* The Scanlons' garden today.

Top: Photograph by Otto Fenn, 1973. Courtesy Sag Harbor Historical Society.

Taking her lead from the gentle overlapping of styles in her Sag Harbor home, antiques dealer Eliza Werner lives with what she likes from an amalgam of periods, mixed with souvenirs from the town's seafaring history and comfortable seating pieces in the beamed study (*top*). The house itself is early nineteenth-century Federal, but the dining room woodwork (*opposite*) shows Greek Revival additions. The Dutch chandelier is hung with *kugels,* German Christmas ornaments. Nineteenth-century spongeware and animal cutting boards are often put to use in the kitchen (*above*).

Once owned by John Alexander Tyler, son of President John Tyler and Julia Gardiner Tyler, the 1836 Greek Revival house at 217 Main Street in East Hampton was "modernized" to Victorian taste at the turn of the century. When the current owner asked architect Robert McKinny Barnes to recapture the home's classic beginnings, he added a new back entrance in the Greek Revival style (*opposite*) and turned an old carriage house into a grand little temple by the pool.

Top: Photograph by Lee Minetree, 1992.

49

GINGERBREAD

The Victorian era burst like a genial surprise onto the East End of Long Island. One moment the old families were plowing, fishing, and going to church as usual, in the company of other families they'd known all their lives. The next moment, or so it must have seemed, the towns were overflowing with "furriners."

Wealthy, social, and genteel, these newcomers, who began visiting The Hamptons in the mid-nineteenth century, were among the first members of America's newly emerging leisure class. The boom following the Civil War had created the money and the time for city dwellers to go scouting the countryside for suitable vacation spots.

Remote — both in distance and ambience — The Hamptons seemed otherworldly to urbanites escaping the noise and bustle of metropolitan centers such as New York and Philadelphia. In a day or so, they could travel back two centuries to the preindustrial world. Behind the modest, shingled houses of The Hamptons, working farms stretched across the low landscape, windmills turned in the ocean breeze, and peace and plenty prevailed. Or so it seemed to those from the city, whose interest in the bucolic was being whipped to a frenzy by nineteenth-century social observers such as Andrew Jackson Downing. Calls echoed from the pulpit and the printed page for a greedy, materialistic America to get back to nature. There — in the fresh air of the woods and farmlands, in gardening and the wholesome, simple outdoor life — they promised, lay the answers to most of the moral problems that had arisen with industrialization.

Finding their way to The Hamptons, these affluent "refugees" were enchanted by both the area and its inhabitants, those solid, hardworking farmers and fishermen. Wary at first of their elegant visitors, the townspeople soon accepted the city folk into their lives — and into their homes. Boardinghouses opened, offering enormous farm breakfasts, midday dinners, and evening tea for the splendid sum of seven dollars a week. Between-meal activities were predictably genteel: excursions to the beach, where rustic arbors offered shady protection from unfashionable suntans, or to the woods for berrying and gathering wild mushrooms.

By 1869 the summer visitors had organized a gathering spot for themselves, the East Hampton Lawn Tennis Club (today's Maidstone Club), and three years later, Charles Peter Beauchamp Jefferys, a civil engineer from Pennsylvania, built the first true summer home in town. Sommariva, meaning "highest point on the shore," rose in full Victorian splendor overlooking Hook Pond, and the rush was on among the visiting gentry to build permanent vacation homes of their own. "Half-homes," a late nineteenth-century writer would call them, "summering places...that may even match the city homes of their owners, but...get every autumn double fastening of the cupboards, and a padlocking of the gates."

What an enchanting "half" the houses and their gardens would soon come to occupy. In its Victorian exuberance, Sommariva (opposite) also inspired the style for many of the houses that followed as the long Victorian period went through its many iterations from the mid-1800s past the turn of the century. It was a happy coincidence in timing. Large, light, and airy, with more than a touch of whimsy, the Victorian house and its colorful garden filled with old-fashioned flowers sets the perfect stage for relaxed summertime living and still informs the essentially holiday spirit that pervades The Hamptons today. □

More than a century's worth of summer visitors have sat in the sunshine and shadows and enjoyed the view from the gracious veranda of Sommariva, built in 1872 overlooking Hook Pond in East Hampton. The angle has changed slightly, though. In 1914 a daughter of the original owner had the house moved a hundred yards or so to the east. The sitting room retains its nineteenth-century perspective, with floral patterns and vintage wicker arranged by designer Mark Hampton around the original mantel and overmantel.

Artist Alfred Thompson Bricher caught the essence of Southampton summer life when he painted *In My Neighbor's Garden* in 1883 (*opposite, above*). The seashell-bordered garden is filled with Victorian favorites: hydrangeas, geraniums, and trumpet vines. Heralded in spring by a Mollis azalea (*Rhododendron Kosterianum* hybrid), a neighboring house now owned by Ann and John Pyne (*opposite, below*) was built in 1860 by Captain Peter Howell, a descendant of Southampton founder Edward Howell. *Above*: Winter puts a sugar-powdering of snow on East Hampton gingerbread.

Alfred Thompson Bricher, *In My Neighbor's Garden,* 1883.
Oil on canvas, 24 x 44. Daniel J. Terra Collection, Terra Museum of American Art,
Evanston, Illinois.

Built in 1871 as a summer home for a Presbyterian minister and much added to over the years, this East Hampton house has a mansard roof, a style rarely found in the area. Beyond the wrought-iron Victorian mourning gate, the allegorical statue of Spring on the terrace celebrates the season with a show of crab apple and dogwood trees.

Top: Photograph courtesy Peter Cooper.

Built as a religious camp in the 1870s, the Heights of Shelter Island is now on New York State's Register of Historic Places, acknowledging the scope of Victorian architectural styles that enliven the little community. To Joanne Creveling and Frank Lookstein, however, the Heights still means spiritual — and visual — refreshment. In rooms cooled by neutral colors, they've assembled a very personal collection of vintage finds, such as the truncated table on the porch (*opposite*) and antique linens in the bedroom (*above*).

In the front parlor (*opposite*), signed charts of local waters from 1890 and wax fruit under a bell jar reference the Victorian heritage of the island retreat. Built for summer use only, the house's uninsulated bones add visual texture to the monochromatic color scheme that unifies a diversity of furnishings. Most undistinguished in provenance — except for the early nineteenth-century French engravings in the library (*above*) — they nonetheless come together with singular style.

Victorians who sought the spiritual benefits of the countryside could find them quite literally in the dunes of Southampton. Built in 1879 with its back to the ocean and overlooking Lake Agawam, St. Andrew's Dune Church drew droves of the righteous on summer Sundays, as recorded (*above*) by artist Alfred Cornelius Howland, ca. 1888. The church was sided in the sturdy shingles long favored throughout the East End. In Sagaponack Lake, a shingled 1860 farmhouse (*opposite*) was trimmed in elaborate architectural gingerbread, now painted dark green by the current owner, Rick Goldstein.

Alfred Cornelius Howland, *St. Andrew's Dune Church,* ca. 1888.
Oil on canvas, 20⅛ x 30⅜. Parrish Art Museum, Southampton, New York;
gift of Mrs. Patrick Valentine.

In sync with the farmhouse beginnings of Goldstein's Victorian house (seen in an old photo, *top*), landscape architect Peter Cooper chose old-fashioned plants and flowers for the garden that flows beside the house. From the side porch, where the owner keeps his collection of old fish lures and toys (*above*), the windows look out on a summer display of blue and white platycodon, bee balm (monarda), purple loosestrife (*Lythrum salicaria*), and swamp sunflowers (*Helianthus augustifolius*), with paths of Tennessee crab orchard stone.

Top: Photograph ca. 1941. Courtesy Pauline Paulson.

Virginia Witbeck's Bridgehampton home started life when the Victorian style was just beginning to flower in the East End. To create an appropriate ambience for the classic furnishings and dramatic dark-light color contrasts she favors, Ms. Witbeck did what many Hamptons homeowners had done in the nineteenth century: she reordered the 1840s exterior (*above*) and added a porch to achieve a Neo-Classic sense of symmetry and balance. Some vestiges of pure Victoriana were too charming to change, however, such as the carpenter gothic stair baluster in the center hall.

Black, white, and redolent all over of classic symmetry, the Witbeck sitting room (*above*) balances fireside chaises with English Regency chairs set against gleaming bare floors. The black-white theme, stated downstairs in the architectural engravings and chair cushions, carries up to the bedroom (*opposite*), where a pair of reading chairs flank a formally swagged window.

Genteel as it may look behind its white picket fence, Arthur Williams's 1874 East Hampton house comes as a surprise inside — unless you know that Williams is a world-traveling antiquarian who lives with some of his most dramatic finds. The better to show them off, he has slicked the rooms all-white, including the old floors. An idea borrowed from 1930s decorator Syrie Maugham, he says, the white background works brilliantly behind the eighteenth-century Irish side table and seventeenth-century Portuguese mirror in the front parlor (*top, opposite*). The dining room table is surrounded by English William and Mary chairs. The birdcage that dominates the living room (*above*) came from Coco Chanel's country home, Williams says. The bookcase dates to the early 1800s; the chairs are Chinese, made in 1860.

Barbara D'Arcy and Kirk White, both well known in the world of furniture and interior design, have created a summer house that has come a long way from its humble beginnings as a gardener's cottage in the nineteenth century. Sparkling white outside, the house is warmed inside with melon tones and the couple's wide-ranging collection of antiques, old things, and sudden impulses. The kitchen (*above*) looks across a terrace shaded by ancient trees with lush borders of hosta. Upstairs, the master bedroom suite (*opposite*) occupies the entire second floor of the East Hampton house.

Graceful new windows open the D'Arcy-White house (*above*) to the East Hampton sunshine and ocean breeze. Their living room, however, could even be called cozy, with its deep colors and antique furnishings. Gathered on the rug that underscores the intimate seating area (*opposite*), chairs range from "proper" Chippendale to a needlepoint zebra print, testimony to the designers' eclectic tastes.

The house and garden Victoria Fensterer calls home — when the garden designer is not out making calls on other people's gardens — started out as two parts: as a former cobbler's shop and a nineteenth-century carriage house in Amagansett. She has given the house a singular Edwardian outlook with an eclectic collection of vintage furnishings (*above*) and filled her own garden with such personal favorites as hydrangeas and honeysuckle.

AESTHETIC

Despite its isolation at the far tip of Long Island, the South Fork did not miss a beat in the rapid evolution of architectural styles during the nineteenth century. Again, it was the worldly summer visitors who introduced the new modes, often superimposing current trends on older structures with little regard for the preexisting local landscape.

Not artists Thomas and Mary Nimmo Moran, however. After renting East Hampton cottages for half a dozen seasons, the well-known couple decided in 1884 to put down permanent roots in the town, building a studio-home with a design heritage that could be traced directly to the Aesthetic movement then in full flower in England. Like the Arts and Crafts reformers to follow, adherents of the Aesthetic movement were the progressives of their time, engrossed in an artistic and moral rebellion against the design excesses of the industrial age. When the Morans traveled to London in 1882, they found artists such as James Abbott McNeill Whistler and William Morris living and working in studio-houses they had built in the movement's preferred Queen Anne style. Picturesque and romantic, with bay windows, jutting towers, and decorative surfaces (the sunflower shone in carved detailing), the Queen Anne style actually had more to do with late Elizabethan and Jacobean design than the version popularized by English architect Richard Norman Shaw and his contemporaries.

The Elizabethan style in more recognizable form also would reappear in the South Fork before the century turned. Swept with Anglophilia in the 1890s, East Hamptonites even wanted to restore their village's original seventeenth-century name, Maidstone, honoring the provenance of its Puritan founders. They settled instead for reviving the Elizabethan cottage style. Architect Joseph Greenleaf Thorp, more noted for his work in the Shingle style, chose the Elizabethan mode when he built a half-timbered cottage for himself in 1893. It and his renovation of an eighteenth-century house on Main Street for new owner J. Harper Poor would spark the ensuing vogue for the Elizabethan idiom. (*Opposite,* the back facade of the Poor house laced with Japanese wisteria in spring.)

Thomas and Mary Nimmo Moran had touched off an earlier fashion for the English-driven Aesthetic style when they returned to East Hampton in 1882 and decided to build The Studio on what had been Dr. Edward Osborn's sheep pasture, overlooking Goose Pond (now Town Pond). Moran drew up the plans himself and incorporated the eclectic collection of architectural oddments he had accumulated: mahogany pillars bought from a razed mansion, a porthole from a derelict ship, even a front door from a demolished house on Broadway with the address *938* worked into its leaded glass panes. (Zealous collectors in an era that adored the exotic, the Morans later brought home a Venetian gondola, said to have belonged to Robert Browning, and in it poled merrily around Hook Pond.)

When the Morans' studio was finished in 1884, it was "the first important summer house to be built in a vernacular or provincial style," according to architect Robert A. M. Stern. He likens the house to a traditional East Hampton barn and believes its shingles and gables "can be said to have set the tone for the summer cottages built in the 1890s."

The Morans certainly set a new tone for the artistic life of the village. Now a National Historic site, and designated by its present owner to become an educational center for young artists in the future, The Studio quickly became a lively gathering spot for the Morans' wide circle of artist friends. They danced in its enormous studio-parlor, presented musicales and poetry readings, and staged costumed tableaux. But they also worked. Thomas Moran consolidated his early fame as a landscape painter, focusing on the East Hampton vistas he found so absorbing. A leader of the revival of etching during the late nineteenth century, Mary Nimmo Moran went on to become the first woman member of the New York Etching Club and the Royal Society of Painter-Etchers in London.

Perhaps it can be said that the life the Morans led in The Hamptons in the 1880s — accomplishing solid artistic work in an atmosphere of sunshine and parties — set the pace that still distinguishes the area today. ◻

Top: Thomas Moran in the garden of The Studio, late 1890s.
Center: Mary Nimmo Moran's garden.
Bottom: The Studio interior. Photographs courtesy East Hampton Library,
East Hampton, New York.

Designed specifically to meet the needs of artists, the Morans' 1884 studio-house was as eccentric as it was functional, with a huge central room (*opposite, bottom*) soaring two stories in the light of a large north window. It was natural that other artists, such as New Yorker Theodore Wores, who painted the house (*above*) in the mid-1880s, should be intrigued. So was the American public after The Studio was publicized in the media of the day. Not only famous artists, the Morans were world travelers and collectors in an age fascinated by the faraway and unexpected. They also were very social; Thomas Moran helped found the Maidstone Club and belonged to New York's Lotos, Century, and Salmagundi clubs. Still, their summers centered on the pleasures of home. Mary Nimmo Moran spent hours among her hollyhocks and chrysanthemums (Thomas Moran in the garden, *top*), and friends who stepped across the vine-draped porch (*center*) could always expect bonhomie in abundance.

Theodore Wores, *Thomas Moran's House (East Hampton, Long Island)*, ca. 1895.
Oil on board, 9 x 12. Collection of Drs. Ben and A. Jess Shenson.

Mary Nimmo Moran, *Dr. E. Osborn's Garden*, 1895.
Oil on canvas, 15½ x 19¾. Courtesy East Hampton Library, East Hampton, New York.

Although he was to look at it for forty summers, the East Hampton landscape never dulled in the eyes of artist Thomas Moran. Given to long walks, cane in hand and beard whipping in the seawinds, he memorized — or sketched in the vibrant watercolors that are collectors' delights today — the scenes he would later capture in oils, working in The Studio. Born in England but raised in the United States and destined to establish his reputation by painting the wonders of this country's unknown West, Moran was forever influenced by two English artists, J. M. W. Turner and John Constable. The latter's stamp is unmistakable in Moran's *Watering Place, East Hampton (above)*. Mary Nimmo Moran, in turn, was influenced by her husband, who first encouraged her to take up etching. The medium would quickly overshadow painting (*Dr. E. Osborn's Garden, opposite,* is one of her few known oils) and win her fame in England as well as America.

Thomas Moran, *The Watering Place, East Hampton,* n.d.
Oil on canvas, 14½ x 26½. Parrish Art Museum, Littlejohn Collection, Southampton, New York.

The slow evolution of architectural styles — from the transplanted English houses of the seventeenth and eighteenth centuries to the Anglophilia of the mid-1890s — can be read under the exterior of the J. Harper Poor house in East Hampton (*above*). Hidden at its core is a house dating to the eighteenth century. In 1911 New York architect Joseph Greenleaf Thorp, who summered and worked in East Hampton, renovated the house as an "Elizabethan cottage," using stucco, carved beams, and small-paned windows to express empathy with the English-inspired Arts and Crafts movement. (*Opposite,* the garden in winter and laden with wisteria in spring.)

In the tradition of nineteenth-century artists who applied the beliefs of the Aesthetic movement to their studio-homes, well-known illustrator Jeremiah Goodman has organized his personal and artistic life in the dependency (*opposite*) that once served as the carriage house to Poor's renovated "Elizabethan cottage." Goodman's studio (*above*) holds part of the eclectic accumulation of furnishings and "props" that gives the house its present-day personality. A container bristles with glass walking sticks; the leaning columns once supported a porch in Sante Fe.

In Goodman's sitting room (*above*), sleek slate floors and a sophisticated interplay of white-and-black create visual coolness just a step away from the sun-soaked garden. Metal stairs spiral like a dramatic sculpture to the rooms upstairs, past a table displaying Japanese pottery and weapons from New Guinea. Goodman's dining room (*opposite*) centers on the large eighteenth-century Dutch armoire. Under a Russian chandelier, a fabric of his own design covers the round dining table.

The bedroom of Goodman's renovated carriage house opens through double glass doors onto the flagstone terrace of his garden (*above*). The architect who recast the house as an "Elizabethan cottage," Joseph Greenleaf Thorp, also chose the style for a summer home he built for himself in 1893. East Hampton's first in the neo-Elizabethan vernacular, the cottage and its perennial garden have long been a popular attraction for village visitors. It was photographed in midsummer (*opposite*) in the 1970s.

Photograph by William Grigsby. Courtesy *House and Garden* magazine.

COTTAGES

Large and eccentric, with playful, arched porches and improbable towers, the Shingle style house proclaims "holiday" at a glance. Pleasurable associations are spontaneous: summer times and summer things — croquet on broad lawns, afternoons in wicker chairs, tea tables towering with cakes, and the laughter of people relaxing on holiday.

That was summer life in the late nineteenth century — at least as it was lived in the seaside resorts of Newport, Maine, and eastern Long Island. Although the Shingle style was high fashion, interpreted by such architects-to-the-gentry as McKim, Mead & White, the houses were built, in the main, with quiet "old money" by owners who euphemized them as "cottages." Never mind that there might be fourteen bedrooms under those gabled roofs; claddings of ordinary weathered shingles diluted any danger of grandiosity. In The Hamptons, moreover, the Shingle style eased the transition between homes in the rich, new summer colonies and the old shingled houses that had already been weathering for two centuries.

Of course, the Shingle style was manifested in other buildings, such as St. Thomas Episcopal Church in Amagansett (*opposite*), and in true cottages. Stanford White applied the style eloquently when he designed the shingled house on the Southampton dunes where his friend William Merritt Chase would summer from 1892 to 1901. The house helped entice Chase to come to the island to direct the plein-air school of painting in Shinnecock, as devoutly wished by local art enthusiasts (led by Mrs. William Hoytt, Mrs. Henry Kirke Porter, and Samuel L. Parrish, who later gave the Parrish Museum to Southampton).

That same year McKim, Mead & White also designed the Shingle style Shinnecock Hills Golf Club, but with his other hand, White was already in touch with the Colonial Revival style his firm would popularize. The Orchard in Southampton (now Whitefield condominium) epitomizes the genre in both the mansion's architecture and its Colonial-inspired gardens. Enveloping an existing farmhouse, White re-created a columned, porticoed "Mount Vernon" for connoisseur and bon vivant James Breese, another close friend. It was to be White's last effort. He left off supervising painters in the music room, the story goes, to return to New York and a fatal encounter with ex-lover Evelyn Nesbit's jealous — and gun-toting — husband, Harry K. Thaw.

The Gilded Age also had its quieter pursuits. Many now-famous gardens were being established in the East End. While grand country mansions elsewhere on Long Island commanded formal, European-style gardens, The Hamptons' gardens were fairly conservative and mostly English, usually larger and more formal in Southampton than in East Hampton. There, the lady of the house often undertook the design of the garden herself — inspired, perhaps, by the prevailing notion that gardening was an art more "feminine" than architecture and, therefore, "suitable" for women. Suit them it did: inventive and inspired, they conquered the "treeless plain" and constant ocean winds. The now ubiquitous privet hedge was one answer to the winds. Another was conjured by Anna Gilman Hill, who designed and enclosed her renowned Grey Gardens in walls of concrete poured by a local mason. Still other intrepid gardeners ventured directly onto the dunes, gradually turning them into lush, flowering landscapes, and into the ponds and marshes to coax extraordinary water gardens into being. A cheerful eccentric of the day, Mrs. Lorenzo G. Woodhouse (later Mrs. Stephen Cummins) reportedly rowed through her lilies at Greycroft in a red boat named "The Swamp Angel." At Georgica Pond, artists/decorators Adele and Albert Herter made gardens on both water and land around the house Grosvenor Atterbury designed for them in 1898. Yet another celebrated East Hampton garden was created by Mary Kennedy Woodhouse as a series of "rooms" outside her 1904 cottage, The Fens. (Mrs. Woodhouse inherited Greycroft, which she dedicated as a nature sanctuary. Later she created the Guild Hall Museum for East Hampton.)

Along with these remarkable amateur gardeners, The Hamptons would nurture some of America's first professional women landscape architects. One of the foremost was Ruth Dean of East Hampton, who championed the use of native East End plants — a radical notion among gardeners who adored the exotic and extravagant. Ruth Dean is remembered today for, among other things, refusing to gild the lily — even in such a gilded age. □

William Merritt Chase. *Chase Homestead, Shinnecock, L.I.,* ca. 1893.
Oil on panel, 16 x 18. San Diego Museum of Art, California.
Gift of Mrs. Walter F. Fisher.

For a decade of summers, while his reputation and his large family thrived, William Merritt Chase lived in the shingled Shinnecock Hills cottage (*above*) designed by Stanford White. Director of the country's first school of open-air painting, Chase attracted a hundred or so students a season. (In the city, he founded the school that would become the New York School of Fine and Applied Arts, later the Parsons School.) Filled with luminous light and the joy of summers from 1892 to 1901, painting after painting captured his own children at play and offered a glimpse of the house itself over the dunes (*opposite*).

William Merritt Chase's home, Shinnecock Hills, ca. 1895. Porch detail, ca. 1908.
William Merritt Chase Archives, Parrish Art Museum, Southampton, New York.

Like his celebrated New York studio on Tenth Street, Chase's studio at Shinnecock (*above*) was filled with sometimes exotic props and reproductions of works by Diego Velázquez, an artist who greatly influenced Chase's art and even aspects of his life. Chase named one of his eight children, daughter Helen Velázquez, in honor of the Spanish painter and occasionally led the family in *tableaux vivants,* a popular entertainment, for which they dressed in costumes to reenact Velázquez's paintings. *Opposite,* daughter Alice, seen as a child on the preceding page, poses in her father's studio under Velázquez's portrait.

Studio interior, photograph ca. 1902. Courtesy William Merritt Chase Archives, Parrish Art Museum, Southampton, New York.

William Merritt Chase, *Alice in Shinnecock Studio,* ca. 1901.
Oil on canvas, 38 x 43. Parrish Art Museum, Littlejohn Collection, Southampton, New York.

One of the most famous American artists of the day — and certainly one of the most dashing in the spats and white boutonnieres he favored — Chase taught both Southampton's summering society and serious artists such as Rockwell Kent, Joseph Stella, and Georgia O'Keeffe. On Mondays Chase conducted public critiques — sometimes to the students' discomfort — and on Tuesdays he took brush in hand (*above*) to offer instruction by example. The many views he recorded of the scene (*opposite, Shinnecock Hills,* ca. 1895) also made the dunes forever famous in American landscape art.

Photograph ca.1892. Courtesy William Merritt Chase Archives,
Parrish Art Museum, Southampton, New York.

William Merritt Chase, *Shinnecock Hills,* ca. 1895.
Pastel on canvas, 16 x 24. Collection of Peter G. Terian.

Photographs by Mattie Edwards Hewitt, ca. 1914. Courtesy Nassau County Museum
Collection, Long Island Studies Institute, Hempstead, New York.

They were hardly birds of a feather, the flamboyant James Breese and Samuel Longstreth Parrish, the cultured and civic-minded son of prominent Philadelphia Quakers who studied and collected what he thought was the best of Old World art. But they both left their imprint on the town of Southampton and, by extension, on the course of American art, architecture, and garden design today. Breese was a dilettante in the best sense of the word, given to fast sports cars and showgirls. But when he asked his friend Stanford White to design his house, it would open the way for the Colonial Revival movement at the turn of the century. White enveloped Breese's eighteenth-century farmhouse in a grand white clapboard building with a Mount Vernon–inspired portico (*opposite, top*). Behind the house, a columned pergola stretched for two hundred feet, past rose and sculpture gardens (*bottom*), before the garden continued in vanishing-point perspective. Parrish's garden of classic sculptures (*above*) may have been more modest in size but not in impact. The museum he founded in 1896 to house it and other works of Italian Renaissance art (in a building designed by Grosvenor Atterbury) has broadened Parrish's original intent to include the entire spectrum of art in America today.

As their first commission in Southampton, McKim, Mead & White designed this three-story shingled house in 1885, wrapping a gracious porch around three sides to take full advantage of the views of Lake Agawam. The architects also flanked the central fireplace with windows in the principal drawing room (*above*) so that on chilly summer evenings, the original owners could enjoy watching a dancing fire in contrast to the lake waters that sparkled in the distance. More than a century later, their legerdemain still charms the room, given fresh sparkle of its own by designer Betty Sherrill, president of McMillen, Inc. Characteristic of the Aesthetic influence of the 1880s, the fireplace shows a flattened sunflower motif on each side. The paneled staircase (*opposite*) leads to more than a dozen bedrooms, not an extravagance in a "cottage" of that gilded era.

Behind the house (seen from the front, *top*), a broad lawn rolls down toward the edge of Southampton's Lake Agawam. In summertime, it is bordered with old-fashioned hollyhocks, standing tall in the distance beyond the comfortable three-sided porch (*above*). When McKim, Mead & White designed the house, they added a special set of stairs to the west side so riders could climb easily on and off their horses. Today's visitors can pass on foot through a garden arch of lush green privet (*opposite*).

Designed in 1893 by Long Island architect I. H. Green, Jr., for Lorenzo G. Woodhouse and his wife, Emma, Greycroft became world renowned for the Japanese water garden Emma fashioned from the large marshy site. (After Woodhouse died, Emma married Stephen Cummins, and the gardens carried his name.) Where Mrs. Cummins was once poled about in her boat, "The Swamp Angel," a nature trail has been created for the village of East Hampton. The house (*above*) was renovated most recently by architect Robert A. M. Stern and decorated for the current owners by Ronald Brick. He lavished chintz on the airy living room (*opposite, top*) and created a sitting room from a spacious stair landing (*below*).

In every room, the Shingle style Greycroft has a fireplace that has been retained through a series of renovations. Fitted with a rotisserie today, the fireplace in the breakfast area is conveniently raised to table height (*opposite*). Across the top march ducks painted on metal, and the hearth showcases a collection of nineteenth-century majolica pitchers with a corn motif. In 1895, the year after the house was built, watercolorist Alice Hirschberg recorded a path (*above*) leading in from the still-bucolic countryside toward East Hampton.

Alice Hirschberg, *Roadway in East Hampton,* 1889.
Watercolor, 9¼ x 14½. Courtesy Guild Hall Museum, East Hampton, New York;
gift of Richard Netter.

Photographs by Mattie Edwards Hewitt, ca. 1924. Courtesy Nassau County Museum
Collection, Long Island Studies Institute, Hempstead, New York.

Her 1915 search for *Beautiful Gardens in America* led author Louise Shelton to East Hampton and the gardens of Mary Kennedy (Mrs. Lorenzo E.) Woodhouse at The Fens. Her rectangular, connecting formal garden was laid out as a series of "rooms," each furnished with ornamental pools, arbors, seats, birdbaths, and patterned beds of petunias, heliotropes, snapdragons, and other annuals. Roses were her signature flower, and Mrs. Woodhouse lavished them over the arches, arbors, and pergolas that linked the "rooms." The garden presented "to the artist's eye a lovely picture of flowers, pool, and arches," which was recorded by pioneering garden photographer Mattie Edwards Hewitt (*opposite, top*, the trellis; *below*, the view back to the trellis). *Above*, the garden years after, reinterpreted and photographed by a later owner, designer Benjamin Baldwin.

Gaines Ruger Donoho, *Woodhouse Water Garden,* 1911.
Oil on canvas, 24 x 34. Courtesy Guild Hall Museum, East Hampton, New York.

Mrs. Stephen S. Cummins's water garden. Photograph ca. 1914. Courtesy East Hampton Library,
East Hampton, New York.

The internationally known garden Mrs. Lorenzo G. Woodhouse created in 1901 from the swamp behind her East Hampton home would prove a bottomless source of inspiration for artist Gaines Ruger Donoho. Encompassing two acres of Oriental flowers, such as irises and water lilies, plus streams, red Japanese bridges, a pond, and two tea houses, the garden lay diagonally across from the house to which Donoho and his wife had moved ten years before. The artist spent hours there, lovingly exploring the riotous colors and textural contrasts for paintings such as *Woodhouse Water Garden* (*opposite*) and *Anemones* (*above*). The Cummins garden (as it would be known after Mrs. Woodhouse was widowed and remarried) is now part of a village nature trail. Another part was donated by Donoho's widow in memory of the natural beauty he found so accessible in East Hampton.

Gaines Ruger Donoho, *East Hampton Garden, Anemones in Foreground,* ca. 1912.
Oil on canvas, 30 x 36. Hirschl & Adler Galleries, New York City.

Sunny colors in the living room, splashed with roses that rival the gardens outside, warm away any hauteur that may have lingered in this landmark Southampton house when designer Betty Sherrill and her family moved in. It was designed in 1899 by Carrère & Hastings for Secretary of War Elihu Root, who named it Mayfair. Betty Sherrill, president of McMillen, Inc., rarely uses the Mayfair name ("a bit pretentious"), but she certainly uses the house to its gracious fullest.

Sparkling white wicker, set against floors painted dark green, imparts a note of crispness to the commodious porch from which Betty Sherrill can survey her favorite place, her gardens. They are arranged, Victorian style, in separate "rooms" threaded through by connecting walks. In her spring garden, some twenty thousand daffodils come joyously into bloom each season. Summers provide the ample armloads of cutting flowers the designer delights in massing for arrangements throughout the house. *Opposite,* her garden room, with racks of gardening hats at the ready.

In love though they were with their villa on the Riviera, the Murphys, Sara (Wiborg) and Gerald, often returned in the 1920s and 1930s to Dunes, her parents' summer house in East Hampton, with its splendid sunken gardens (*above*). Inspired living today: Betty Sherrill's blue and white dining room (*opposite*) in Southampton.

Top: Photograph by Mattie Edwards Hewitt, the Wiborg garden, view of Hook Pond, ca. 1924.
Courtesy Nassau County Museum Collection, Long Island Studies Institute, Hempstead, New York.
Bottom: Hand-colored postcard showing the Frank B. Wiborg residence and gardens, ca. 1920.
Courtesy East Hampton Library, East Hampton, New York.

Photograph by Mattie Edwards Hewitt, 1923. Exedra, gate, and thatched toolshed.
Courtesy Nassau County Museum Collection, Long Island Studies Institute,
Hempstead, New York.

When she set out in 1914 to coax her famed Grey Gardens from the rough pasture of bayberries near the sea in East Hampton, Anna Gilman Hill knew just what she wanted: "cement walls high enough in some places to be pierced by arches with clanging wooden doors ... arches recessed in the wall for seats and a fountain ... a thatched tool house ... an exedra overlooking the sea." Mrs. Hill engaged a village carpenter and mason to realize her vision, filling her walled garden with flowers in pale colors and plants with gray foliage to complement "the soft gray of the dunes, cement walls, and sea mists." Later owned by John "Black Jack" Bouvier's sister and her daughter (aunt and cousin of Jacqueline Bouvier Kennedy Onassis), the house and garden have been brought back to bloom by current owners Sally Quinn and Ben Bradlee. Their garden room (*above*) overlooks the walled garden. *Opposite*, Mrs. Hill's exedra and the newly landscaped pool today.

Looking back in *Forty Years of Gardening,* the book she wrote in 1938, Anna Gilman Hill remembered the pleasures of sitting in her Grey Gardens (the exedra, *top*): "You had a glimpse of blue water between dunes, high dunes, grass-covered and soft gray, like our walls. . . . In this friendly little place I realized my ideal." Asked to revive and expand upon Mrs. Hill's ideal, landscape designer Victoria Fensterer added old roses (Betty Prior), mimosa trees, *Cryptomeria japonica,* and Pfitzer juniper (*opposite*). She brought in an ancient peegee hydrangea to plant beside the new pool and created a cool, intimate herb garden (*above*).

Top: Photograph by Mattie Edwards Hewitt, 1923. Looking through the rose-decked exedra to the sea. Courtesy Nassau County Museum Collection, Long Island Studies Institute, Hempstead, New York.

Looking down Lily Pond Lane today, you can see the distinctive East Hampton blue trim of Grey Gardens in the distance (second house from the right). The covered gate leads to another garden in which serpentine hedges of privet enclose armfuls of colorful annuals. As Anna Gilman Hill once observed about the rich, glacial soil and moist sea air of The Hamptons, "Gardening in Suffolk County spoils you for gardening in North America. It is an almost foolproof place."

In the spirit of the summer holiday life for which they were planned, rooms in Hamptons cottages often opened directly onto gracious outdoor terraces. Gardens offered benches, pergolas, and other intimate areas from which the landscaping could be enjoyed at leisure. In the garden surrounding Augusta Maynard's Southampton house, a flagstone terrace (*top*) displays Japanese iris, lobelia, and a variety of rock plants nestled between its flagstones. The garden also features nearly three dozen full-grown trees that she had moved from a former garden in Bridgehampton, all of which survived.

Plantings designed by Victoria Fensterer enhance the pergola (*opposite*) of an East Hampton cottage that once belonged to John Vernon Bouvier, grandfather of Jacqueline Bouvier Kennedy Onassis, and later to Abstract Expressionist painter Adolph Gottlieb. The terraced garden designed by Peter Cooper for another East Hampton cottage (*above*) is planted with fifteen varieties of hydrangeas, lavender, bee balm (monarda), purple loosestrife (*Lythrum*), Russian sage (*Perovskia*), and coneflowers (*Echinacea*). Overlooking the ocean, the 1924 house was renovated in 1927 by architect Grosvenor Atterbury, who spent his summers in Southampton.

It was a homecoming, literally, when Susan and Charles Bullock bought their 1928 stucco cottage in East Hampton. She had spent the summers of her childhood under its tiled roof and playing in its gardens. Now reordered to her grown-up perspective, the gardens include a round of vegetables (*opposite, top*), centered with a sundial and bisected with brick walks for easy picking. Tubs of tropical hibiscus guard the gateway into the garden (*opposite, below*). At the front entrance (*above*), treillage painted the same East Hampton blue as the house trim presides over a dooryard garden filled with white petunias, black-eyed Susans, and Betty Prior roses.

Two venerable centers of South Fork social life, Southampton's Shinnecock Club (*top*) and East Hampton's Maidstone Club, were both designed by the leading architects of their day. In 1892 McKim, Mead & White created the Shingle style Shinnecock, the second golfing club in America. The story of the Maidstone Club must be told in three chapters: the shingled club was twice designed by Long Island architect I. H. Green, Jr., and twice built between 1892 and 1922. Both burned. The present club (*above*), built in 1922, is the work of architect Roger Bullard. Artist member Childe Hassam recorded the action in 1926 (*opposite*).

Top: Photograph courtesy Southampton Historical Society.

Childe Hassam, *Morning on the Maidstone Links, the Fifteenth Green,* 1926.
Oil on canvas, 18 x 25½. American Academy of Arts and Letters.

The press has labeled interior designer Mark Hampton a "Renaissance man," homage paid to his prowess as author and decorator for the nation (projects have included the White House, Blair House, and the first family's homes). In Southampton, all that is forgotten. The house Hampton chose to remodel started out as a small, shingled gardener's cottage on Consuelo Vanderbilt Balsan's large estate, Garden Side. The designer added a two-story wing but has retained the house's relaxed attitude. *Opposite,* the Hamptons' classic rose garden. *Above,* painted Gothic Revival wrought iron is silhouetted against the pool house shingles.

Hampton has used what he calls "one of those Billy Baldwin/Albert Hadley color schemes" in the large living room of the cottage. He describes the deep brown walls, played off against white and beige, as "shadowy" in summer and "wonderful in winter," when the family manages to get there for off-season holidays. By contrast, the dining room (*above*) is in several tints of pale sunshine, the lightest used to pick out the moldings. The blue-and-white china is part of a huge collection — Hampton says he believes in impulse buying. He disapproves of frills and fussy things for vacation houses. Neither is anywhere to be found in this cottage.

As playful as it is imposing, this large Southampton house has been imbued with a perpetual holiday mood by designer David Easton and landscape architect George Betsill. Exterior walls, painted soft pink, embrace the rose garden Betsill framed in box and centered on a sundial at the entryway (*above*). *Opposite,* from the house's grand entrance forward, Easton's design for the interiors evokes the splendid whimsy of Brighton, with faux painted bamboo treillage on the walls and faux parquet floors. Large, pink tin lanterns and soft pink planters bring both the color theme and the alfresco attitude into the house itself.

Graced with French doors that open out onto the rose garden, the sitting room (*opposite, bottom*) echoes the soft apricot-pink and blued green that distinguish the exterior of the house. The carpet is needlepoint, in the English Regency style. Applied green trelliswork wraps the lower walls in the dining room (*opposite, top*), where the owner has chosen to display her amusing collection of chicken paintings. The chandelier is tin with porcelain flowers. In the large drawing room (*above*), Easton has spread nineteenth-century Bessarabian rugs over sisal carpeting to organize the seating groups and give the room a pleasant intimacy.

The world's first professional interior decorator, Elsie de Wolfe (later Lady Mendl) would applaud the interior garden ambience of this pool house, designed by architect Tom Kirchoff for a venerable 1928 Southampton cottage. It was Elsie de Wolfe who made lavish use of garden trelliswork in America's most fashionable homes early in this century. In the same classic spirit, English designer Georgina Fairholme has paired treillage with simple white fabrics inside the pool house. Outside, the garden itself is all white, even to the green-and-white variegated hollies.

The cottage's wicker-filled garden room has splendid views of two vistas — the sunken rose garden just outside the French doors and the romantic view that has been painted through the faux stone arch by artist Robert Jackson. Jackson also painted a trompe l'oeil sky on the ceiling of the room to further the alfresco ambience planned by the designer. Planted in segments according to color, the sunken rose garden itself was originally created in 1928 by Annette Hoyt Flanders, a renowned early landscape designer.

Among the treasures gathering dust in the attic of this Colonial Revival farmhouse in Wainscott, today's owner found a photograph of the 1895 house, standing tall and alone against its fields. In the century since, the farmland has grown up and softened into graceful contours, with recent help from landscape architect Thomas Reinhardt. *Top,* some of the twenty-six thousand daffodils in the early-spring garden.

The new owner has brought his own treasures to the attic (*above*), which has been opened up to the ocean view through an arched window added by architect Fred Stelle. Working with Annabelle Selldorf, Stelle painted the entire space white as background for a collection of old pieces, including the chair table that stands against the chimney. *Opposite,* Old Windsor comb-back chairs mix with reproductions around a trestle table in the new glass breakfast room Stelle attached off the farmhouse kitchen. On the deck that runs through the glass walls, an herb garden flourishes in individual clay pots.

147

Without entirely abandoning its former role, the summer kitchen that served the old farmhouse has taken on new life as the owner's pool house. Moved to its new location, the renovated building (*opposite*) is outfitted with a brick barbecue for cooking poolside. It also houses the sauna. Revamping the landscape in another fashion, Thomas Reinhardt contoured the fields surrounding the farmhouse to create natural backgrounds for extensive plantings of Siberian iris (*Iris sibirica*) and native *Iris Pseudacorus*. Brightening the drive (*above*), *Coreopsis verticillata* (Zagreb and Moonbeam).

The exterior of Mel Dwork's small, pre–World War II house creates ordinary expectations. Inside, however, something extraordinary has happened. All the walls have vanished; all the dividers have disappeared. Where many tiny rooms were once squeezed onto two floors, a single space now soars to the open rafters. The designer uses area rugs, low standing screens, and a bookcase-backed kitchen island (*opposite*) to demarcate activities within the room. The signature sofa-cum-bed is Dwork's own design. *Above,* a painted English country Chippendale chest anchors one corner in the unispace.

Reclaiming early Americana piece by piece, magazine editor Durrell Godfrey and her husband, art director John Berg, are slowly crowding themselves out of their colorful, but tiny, East Hampton cottage. Their collection of quilts (*opposite*) stages a riot of pattern in its bookshelf. Other quilts are hung as background for an ingathering of folk furniture, art, and oddments from their constant foraging in flea markets, yard sales, and junk stores. Living in a boathouse (*above*) keeps John McMahon within easy reach of his passion, sailing. The architect (he's with the design firm of Parish-Hadley) and his wife, Mary Anne, enjoy a wraparound view of West Neck Bay on Shelter Island. Three sides of the boathouse consist entirely of windows.

Top: Autochrome by Frances Benjamin Johnston, 1927.
Bottom: Adele Herter's formal garden. Photograph courtesy Nassau County Museum
Collection, Long Island Studies Institute, Hempstead, New York.

The Creeks in East Hampton has had only two owners in its history, but they were more than enough to win its place in the annals of outstanding American gardens. Both were artists, both visionary gardeners, both as different as their times. In 1913, The Creeks was a wedding gift (from his wealthy parents) to Albert and Adele Herter, young artists who had met in fin de siècle Paris. He'd known the area as a boy, but the couple set out to know it intimately — in different seasons, by the light of different moons — camping out at various locations for months before finally choosing the site for the Italianate villa Grosvenor Atterbury designed in 1899. Around it, the Herters created an Italian-inspired garden so vast it required the attention of thirty-five Japanese gardeners, who were housed in tents during the summer season. *Opposite,* The Creeks in the 1920s. *Above,* looking across Georgica Pond today.

Alfonso Ossorio saw The Creeks through very different eyes — those of a Surrealist artist, of a visionary who would nurture the avant-garde, especially the work of friend Jackson Pollock. It was to visit Pollock that Ossorio first came to the East End. In 1952 he bought The Creeks from the Herters' son, Christian A. Herter (secretary of state in the Eisenhower administration), and set about imposing his highly personal vision on both the house and the gardens. He painted the former black — a better background for the art, explains Ted Dragon, Ossorio's longtime companion (the artist died in 1991). The gardens responded as dramatically to the new aesthetic, as Ossorio resculpted the landscape using conifers as his principal medium. "He planted trees exactly the way he would do a congregation or a painting," Ted Dragon says. The fifty-seven acres at The Creeks are punctuated with Ossorio's sculptures, many made of found objects, set against what the American Conifer Society has called "a living work of art." *Opposite,* the entrance to the house; sculptures among the trees. *Above,* the swimming pool as Ossorio saw it.

Teeming with energy and with the unexpected, Ossorio's congregations have been called "an important, nearly all-purpose footnote to the history of postwar art," expressing as they do elements of Surrealism, Abstract Expressionism, and assemblage art. As complex, perhaps, as his work, Ossorio himself is remembered as erudite and gracious. Heir to a sugar fortune in the Philippines, he was educated in England, studied at Harvard, and became a U.S. citizen in 1939. Ossorio turned The Creeks into a center for artistic and social activity, bringing together many artists who were making New York — and, by extension, The Hamptons — the vital center of the art world in the mid-twentieth century. *Above* and *opposite:* Ossorio's studio, with his own work and a display of animal horns, part of his vast collections of disparate objects.

MODERN

When Jackson Pollock and Lee Krasner were married in October 1945, their wedding not only presaged a new era in The Hamptons, but it also reflected much of what had gone before. This most Bohemian of couples in the New York art world had decided to give up the Eighth Street studio they'd shared for three years and move to the far tip of Long Island; to the little community of The Springs, not far from East Hampton; to what Lee, at least, considered a conventional small town. An unmarried couple, even a couple of artists, would raise eyebrows, she reasoned.

No doubt Lee was right. By 1945 The Hamptons had more or less settled back into the remote and staid society it had once been. The upheavals of the century to date had seen to that. The Great Depression had slowed, then reversed, the development of the resort community. Some of the big houses had been razed; others had been lost to fires. A series of spectacular storms in the 1930s had destroyed other buildings and drastically altered the landscape. Summer life had diminished, then gas rationing during World War II had all but isolated The Hamptons from New York City, which had been the driving force in its earlier development.

The year they were married (in Marble Collegiate Church on Fifth Avenue), the Pollocks moved to a farmhouse in The Springs with a barn and five acres (*opposite*, the studio floor today), bought with a loan from Peggy Guggenheim (to be repaid with the proceeds from Pollock's paintings). Their odyssey together would end tragically eleven years later when Pollock's car crashed into a tree on Fireplace Road. But they had helped usher in the new era in The Hamptons.

Artists attracted artists, as they had done in the nineteenth century when The Tile Club first "discovered" the quiet little backwater. Willem and Elaine de Kooning and Grace Hartigan soon followed Pollock and Krasner to The Hamptons. Alfonso Ossorio visited in 1949 and returned in 1952 to live and work at The Creeks on Georgica Pond. From Europe came artists dislodged by the war, among them the Surrealist Max Ernst, who summered in East Hampton in the 1940s. American artists such as Robert Motherwell, Jim Dine, and Larry Rivers also arrived. Fairfield Porter came and stayed, in Southampton, from 1949 until his death in 1975 (much of his work is now in the Parrish Art Museum).

Just as members of The Tile Club had done in the nineteenth century, many artists in this new wave were seeking an escape from New York. While Abstract Expressionism may have been born in the city, it certainly spent its summers in the East End. For four remarkable years, the avant-garde also had its own showcase in an East Hampton shop front that became the Signa Gallery (Ossorio was one of the founders). Among the artists who showed there were Krasner, Pollock, both de Koonings, Motherwell, Rivers, and Balcomb Greene. Following a now well-established scenario, Greene had come to the East End to paint and ended up staying. In 1947 he bought an abandoned World War II dugout on the bluffs of Montauk, where he designed and built a house for himself.

Artist Robert Gwathmey left the house building to his son, architect Charles Gwathmey. It was to be a landmark decision, not only in the course of house design in the East End but also in American residential architecture. The cool, minimal, Modernist house Gwathmey created in Amagansett for his parents was to signal a sea change in the architectural future of The Hamptons. The 1966 house recast the spirit of holiday in new and abstract terms that owed nothing to either the architectural vocabulary of the old resort area or even to its natural surroundings.

But it was as invigorating as the new art that was now being made in studios throughout the area. It also was contagious. Suddenly the dunes and potato fields were punctuated with abstract expressions in architecture, many of them highly inventive and experimental in design. Again in the mid-twentieth century, the South Fork became *the* mecca for new ideas. Only this time it was architects who attracted architects. And unlike the painters of an earlier era, few of them would have been interested in visiting Payne's "Home, Sweet Home," that shingled relic of an altogether different architectural world. □

Jackson Pollock resisted when Lee Krasner suggested a move to the remote East End of Long Island. Changing his mind would change his art. Coming from a drab Greenwich Village tenement into the sunshine and space of The Springs opened a new range of colors and led to Pollock's hallmark technique: pouring paint onto canvases laid on the studio floor. Already a successful painter when they met, Lee took over the barn-studio after Pollock's death. Both left a colorful imprint. When the State University of New York at Stony Brook renovated the property as an artists' study center, a layer of flooring was pulled up, revealing the vivid palimpsest.

Balcomb Greene explored a number of intellectual avenues before coming to painting. Philosophy student, Dartmouth College English professor, and (unpublished) writer of fiction, Greene finally discovered painting in pre–World War II Paris. Back in New York, where he received a master's degree in art, Greene became one of the first artists to move to the East End in the 1940s. High above the breakers of Montauk, he designed and built the cement-walled house (*opposite*) from which he could look directly onto the seascapes that had become his new fascination.

Balcomb Greene, *Sails and White Cliffs,* 1978.
Oil on canvas, 48 x 60. Collection of John C. Waddell.

Born from the bluffs and built with the help of his students, Greene's flat-roofed house was designed to grow naturally from its rugged site, an abandoned dugout that had been used as a lookout during the Second World War. *Above,* a French butcher's table, set on the brick floors Greene used to further his all-natural design, holds a collage made in 1938 by the artist's first wife, the late Gertrude Greene. Greene himself made the metal ship's weather vane (*opposite*) that overlooks the view down the bluffs from the house, a scene that influenced many of the artist's paintings.

When twenty-seven-year-old Charles Gwathmey designed this elegantly spare house and studio for his parents in 1966, it would send shock waves across the fields of Amagansett that were felt far beyond the East End. An "instant icon," the house put The Hamptons on the cutting edge of the Modern movement, opening the way for the often experimental designs that followed. Fabric designer Rosalie Gwathmey, widow of the painter Robert Gwathmey, created the still life (*above*) with beach pebbles and a bouquet of catnip.

Serene in its simplicity, the Gwathmey house is sheathed outside in gray-painted wood. Inside, natural wood walls become background for such modern classics as the Corbusier sofa and Breuer chairs in the large living room (*top* and *opposite*). Laid on the horizontal, the paneling flows past a ribbon window in the dining space and out onto the exterior (*above*). Today Charles Gwathmey says that the house, a "unique proposition" at the time, can now be considered "part of The Hamptons vernacular and is as legitimate a point of view here as the old Shingle style."

Top: The Gwathmey house when it was originally completed.
Photograph courtesy Gwathmey / Siegel & Associates.

Fairfield Porter, *Studio Interior,* 1951.
Oil on canvas, 35¾ x 42. Mickelson Gallery, Washington, D.C.

"I do not look for places to paint," artist Fairfield Porter once said. "A place means a lot to me ... because I can't help it." Southampton was such a place. Porter spent more than a quarter of a century there, from 1949 to his death in 1975, painting its landscapes and seascapes in the quiet, always representational style he retained even though Abstract Expressionism was swirling all around him. Porter, also an art editor and critic, gathered a wide circle of friends in the large house on Main Street he shared with poet Anne Channing and their five children. His family was another frequent subject of his paintings. *Above,* the artist and Anne in his studio, shown in his painting, *opposite.*

Photograph courtesy Parrish Art Museum, Southampton, New York;
gift of the estate of Fairfield Porter.

173

Designed in 1967 for a young couple and their children, architect Richard Meier's angular wood house has a monumental mien far beyond its actual size. The brilliant white walls, rising sharply from the ground in deliberate counterpoint to the East Hampton landscape, were a new aesthetic for an area long accustomed to the visual softness of gardens and weather-grayed shingles. Also unexpected is the stroke of pure color that adds a playful note in the light-washed living room (*opposite*).

Photographs by Ezra Stoller, 1970, © Esto.

Recasting the older East Hampton building that originally housed the Jewish Center of The Hamptons, in 1988, architect Norman Jaffe used the familiar Shingle idiom to modern advantage (*above*). Water is his medium at the East Hampton home of Jeff and Patricia Tarr (*opposite*). Here the architect created two bodies of water for the house he designed of Tennessee crab orchard stone: a swimming pool bordered in the same stone and the terraced water garden. Landscape designer Peter Cooper has harmonized the pool areas with plantings that include corkscrew willows.

Discoveries abound in The Hamptons. At times they surprise — like sculptor Bill King's twenty-eight-foot *Irene* (*opposite*) on the East Hampton dunes at namesake Irene Towbin's house, and *Frigid Bather,* made by Hilda Steckel to hesitate forever alongside Barbara Slifka's pool in Bridgehampton (*top*), where landscape architects James van Sweden and Wolfgang Oehme designed the garden. At other times discoveries come quietly — like the medley of greens at the house Robert McKinny Barnes designed for Barbara and Stanley Arkin (*above*). At poolside, landscape architect Peter Cooper has planted blue fescue (*Festuca ovina*), ribbon grass (*Phalaris arundinacea*), and plume grass (*Erianthus ravennae*).

When Larry Rivers wanted an "instant garden," gratification was as close as the artist's Southampton studio: he simply went in and painted himself the lush green trees (*opposite*) that turn his garden into an experience where the real and surreal coexist in great good humor. Although his trees are painted on wood, Rivers also renders more natural landscapes in his signature style, a similar melding of the abstract and the representational. *Above, Last Landscape, Bridge-hampton,* painted in 1959, six years after he moved from New York City.

Larry Rivers, *Last Landscape, Bridgehampton,* 1959.
Oil on canvas, 34 x 47. Collection of the artist.

The Hamptons first came into Larry Rivers's life the year he and artist friend Helen Frankenthaler visited Jackson Pollock in The Springs. It was 1951, Rivers's art studies at New York University were coming to a close, and that trip, he said, planted the first thoughts of leaving the city for the country. One season in a rented cottage confirmed the idea. The next year he moved to Southampton, where his house is now landmarked by the gargantuan pair of formed fiberglass legs striding across the lawn by his studio (*opposite*). In the studio (*top*) are works in progress from his series "Art and the Artist," including (*above*) *Léger and the Final Painting*.

The summer she spent on her knees designing walkways for her medieval herb garden, Margaret "Marggy" Kerr found her unusual new medium — the bricks she now weaves into monotone "rugs." The artist has made her "site sculptures" for private home foyers, East Hampton's town hall, and gardens such as the one she shares in The Springs with husband Robert Richenburg, an Abstract Expressionist who created the rock garden (*opposite*) on the deck of the house designed by Peter Price. In their dining room (*above*), Richenburg's self-portrait and air sculptures of tin and of wire.

Inspired by the "warmth, subtle color variation," and long history of brick, Kerr wrapped her garden of medieval plants (*opposite*) with walkways laid out in intricate patterns that were initially inspired by rugs in her collection, one a Baluch, the other an Ersari Turkoman Katchli. Now the French-born artist, who says she grew up with "threadbare" Oriental rugs, works by inspiration directly on her "canvas," seldom planning designs on paper first. She uses both the smooth face of the brick and the rougher side surfaces to interpret fringes, borders, and geometric details (*above*).

As baronial in size as any grand country seat of yesteryear, an oceanfront house designed by architects Bates, Booher and Lund couches the holiday spirit in modernist terms of smooth, white stucco walls with rounded edges. Inside, designer Mel Dwork balanced antiques with contemporary works, such as the painting by David Ligare on a clear turquoise wall in one bedroom (*above*). Landscape architect Lisa Stamm chose colorful classics, mixing espaliered pear trees, sedum Autumn Joy, and artemesia along the pool area.

It was a tract house, pure and simple — and boring — until designer Benjamin Baldwin took it on. Built in the 1950s, its street-facing garage doors lacked only the proverbial basketball net to complete the anywhere-in-middle-America image. Baldwin delights in metamorphoses (an earlier challenge involved property with the foundation of a demolished house that he turned into an extraordinary sunken garden). Here he streamlined the kitchen, punctuated by a Matisse print (*above*), and redefined the low ceiling in the living room to expand the space visually (*opposite*). Seen through the ranch-style windows, bamboo in the front garden emulates a painted Chinese screen. The actual painting is *The Bridge* by Robert Natkin.

Baldwin's East Hampton house came with an everyday yard — the kind that plays host to a thousand jungle gyms from coast to coast. On that nondescript space, he has superimposed a highly individualistic vision of a garden, composed of twenty-five arbors (*opposite*) arched over with clematis Sweet Autumn (*Maximowicziana*). At his previous home, which had been part of the Woodhouse estate, Baldwin created his garden around and inside the brick walls that remained of the basement of the razed house. *Above, top,* that all-white garden in spring. *Below,* a favorite peach tree in bloom.

Even the dunes that undulate so naturally around Jack Lenor Larsen's Long House in East Hampton have been carefully coaxed to fit the textile artist's new vision. After a quarter century in his nearby Round House (inspired by an African village), Larsen foresaw this space as molten and flowing but *ordered,* nonetheless, to ordain a place for everything that makes up his eclectic life, including large parties with dancing outdoors, his personal loom, and studio (*opposite*). Part Shinto shrine, part big-city loft, Long House rises in a fifteen-acre park that harbors monochromatic flower gardens and sculpture. Twenty-two-foot-tall columns frame the view of a pond where swans idle. Inside, every level is suffused with natural light . . . and Eastern calm.

Like the piano nobile of an Italian villa, the central floor of Long House is raised to gain views of the surrounding park. In the large living room, Robert Clark's sculpture *Excelsior!* spirals toward the twenty-four-foot-high ceiling (*opposite*). Sliding doors open and close to define spaces in the dining room (*top*), where part of Larsen's large collection of primitive and ethnographic art is on view. The display continues in a sitting room on the terrace level (*above*) of Long House, which was designed with architect Charles Forbert.

"It's like a painting that's still being done," artist Robert Dash observes of the garden he has loved, struggled with, reshaped and rethought, and reshaped yet again in the twenty-five years since he moved to Sagaponack. Madoo, he calls his house and its garden, which sprawls over nearly two acres not far from the ocean. But Madoo is never done — will never be done — although it occupies its creator through long working days in season, and fills his winter dreams deciding what comes next. This year, the arch into the garden gleams yellow against the purple columbine (*opposite*). Elsewhere, stairs rise — a vivid surprise — over columbine and sweet woodruff (*Asperula odorata*).

Robert Dash, *Spring II,* 1963.
Oil on canvas, 70 x 50. Private collection.

The art of the garden and the art of the studio are two separate entities, Dash says, but each nourishes the other. Like all his paintings, *Spring II* (*opposite*) represents many gardens, whereas Madoo, the garden, is a painterly composition of textures, colors, forms, and light. "The contemporary garden is [like] an exhibition of paintings or a collection . . . we can move at will," Dash once wrote. *Above,* two views of his collection — Solomon's seal (*Polygonatum biflorum*) with ajuga and a garden path bordered in box leading past white bleeding heart. Chemicals are not allowed in Dash's garden; visitors are. More will come in the future: Madoo has been accepted by The Garden Conservancy, which undertakes to preserve outstanding examples of America's gardening art.

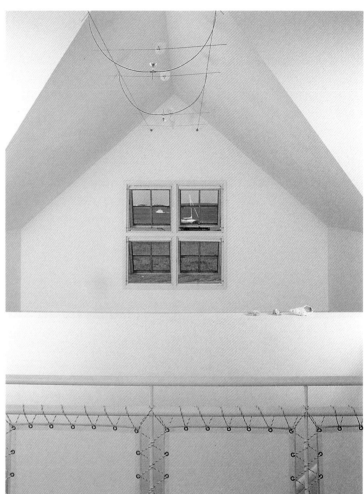

Incorporating an old barn he had moved from a roadside, architect Fred Stelle has created a house outside Sag Harbor that makes subtle reference to the nautical legacy of the area. Small, square porthole windows, like those in the living room (*opposite*), are a repeated motif. Upstairs, railings on the stairway leading to the master bedroom are lashed with canvas. The house is located on Shelter Island Sound, and almost every window affords a water view. The Stelles' own boat is framed (*above*) in the windows of the bedroom, under a "Ya Ya Ho" halogen light.

Jane Freilicher, *View over Mecox (Yellow Wall)*, 1991.
Oil on linen, 80 x 70. Courtesy Fischbach Gallery, New York City.

Artist Jane Freilicher has a double vision of two natural East End attractions from her airy studio in Water Mill. Through the windows on one side, the vista is toward Mecox Bay. Turn in the other direction, and there's the ocean. Freilicher has committed both views to canvas after canvas since the late 1950s, when she and her husband found the house that's their frequent escape from New York City. *Opposite,* her *View over Mecox. Above,* a work table in the studio. When artist Fairfield Porter first introduced them to The Hamptons, the area was still undiscovered and unspoiled. Today Freilicher says she worries that her paintings may one day become "documents of a vanished era."

Known for the ever-changing views she paints from her studio windows (of the ocean, *opposite, top,* and of Mecox Bay, *bottom*), Jane Freilicher often includes bouquets fresh from her own garden in her works. (She arranged the flowers for these photographs.) However, there are times in The Hamptons when it's not even necessary to have a private garden in order to enjoy things fresh from the countryside. Roadside folk art (*above*) is part of the annual spring tradition.

POST-MODERN

In an area as hard by the sea as the South Fork of Long Island, becalmed might be an appropriate word for the spirit that settled over many architects at work there in the 1980s. After two decades or so of daring experimentation with the radically new, they paused for a second look at the old architecture that had distinguished The Hamptons for three centuries and more.

A major inspiration for that backward glance was the new concern for the environment that has been gaining momentum as the century dwindles. It was not only the natural environment that came under siege after a period of enthusiastic building on the dunes and in the potato fields. The *built* environment of the past three hundred years also seemed in danger of being lost in the angular shadows of the Modernists' houses ... until architects began taking a second look at the lean-tos and shingles of the eighteenth and nineteenth centuries and saw much worth quoting in the twentieth century.

Robert A. M. Stern, perhaps the bellwether of this Post-Modern movement, calls it "making peace with the environment. . . . Every building is a comment on the architecture that has come before it." Stern's own "commentary" can be seen in Calf Creek, a 1987 house he designed in Water Mill (*opposite*). "Commenting" on the past is not the same as quoting it verbatim, he emphasizes. "Reviving" and "reinvigorating tradition" are more accurate descriptions of Post-Modern objectives.

Among the traditions revived and reinvigorated are shingles, Palladian-style windows, columns, and other classic motifs that deftly blur the distinction between newly built Post-Modern houses and authentic Shingle style cottages. A story told by the owners of a newly built Post-Modern house illustrates the point. They razed an old house on Great Peconic Bay, then had Robert Stern design a rambling new home that "quoted" liberally from the vernacular Shingle style. Visitors touring the premises soon after the house was completed fondly "remembered" being there as children.

Quoting from the past was heard in whispers as early as 1955, when architects George Nelson and Gordon Chadwick designed a simplified, abstract house in East Hampton and covered its exterior in traditional shingles. Also bridging the past and present, architect Jaquelin T. Robertson adapted the early lean-to idiom for an abstract house designed in 1980, similarly clad in shingles.

As the return to the traditional vernacular has gained momentum, there has been a concurrent movement to restore and remodel many old homes in sympathy with their environment. Often it has been the homeowner who has mandated this return to tradition, much as East Hampton, especially, was swept early in the century by a desire to reclaim its seventeenth-century roots. Now, as then, that desire has been fanned by the social and political tumult of the times that makes the familiar look comfortable and comforting. Where brilliant, leading-edge Modern offered an intellectual challenge, the more rounded edges and more human scale of Post-Modern promises warmth and relaxation. The Modernists sought to create universally valid designs that would be able to exist independently of their environment. By contrast, the site-sensitive Post-Modern house has sparked renewed interest in another cherished tradition — gardens and gardening. Porches also are back among the pleasures of summer after their banishment in the name of Modernism, which, Robert Stern points out, often ignored "the lessons that the traditional summer cottages had to offer, with their orientation to breezes [and] porches."

But then, breezes and porches were part of what started it all, back when the first holiday seekers sought out the far tip of Long Island. They, like today's Post-Modernists, wanted to touch base with tradition, to be "revived and reinvigorated," and most of all to find a place in which they could be happily becalmed.   □

The line between indoors and out is lost in the brilliant light that pours into the dining room of Sunstone, a 1987 house created in his trademark idiom by Post-Modern architect Robert A. M. Stern. The shingled exterior of the house is punctuated with an amplitude of windows to take full advantage of the view overlooking Shinnecock Bay. The view indoors has been designed by Albert Hadley, of Parish-Hadley Associates, in *his* comfortably elegant style, augmented by pots of sunflowers. The pool house (*above*) punctuates the garden, designed by Adele Mitchell and bright in spring with tulips framed in boxwood.

A classic configuration restated by Thomas Jefferson in the eighteenth century and championed in the nineteenth by reformer Orson Squire Fowler, hexagonal shapes add a sense of whimsy to Stern's design for Sunstone in the twentieth. In the bedroom (*top*), the angled walls are articulated with oval windows set above French doors opening onto the panoramic view. Here, and in the corresponding living room hexagon (*below*), Albert Hadley based his airy designs on a palette of soft monotones, focused here and there with bright fabrics and darker woods. The hexagonal library (*opposite*) is a different color story, told in deep shades and clubby patterns.

Overlooking the waters that flowed into a kettlehole left by the retreating glaciers of the Ice Age, architect Thierry Despont has created a warm Post-Modern home in Bridgehampton for Shirley and Jack Silver. Despont defined the exterior with wood, now mellowed to gray on the covered porch (*opposite, bottom*). The kitchen (*top*) also enjoys the water view. In keeping with the easy-living ambience of the house, interior designer T. Keller Donovan used joyous print fabrics on the porch wicker, then softened the color palette in the living room (*above*), where plump, comfortable seats are gathered, front and center, to take in the scenery.

One lovely thing leads to another in the series of gardens planned by landscape architect Lois Sherr for a Post-Modern house in Wainscott. The linear display of perennials (*opposite*) lies beyond a more formal, English-style rose garden and serves as a transition to a cutting garden, which, in turn, leads to the natural meadow with its view of Wainscott Pond. A welcome sitting area, the arbor of rustic timbers (*above*) is covered with Japanese wisteria.

The outdoors is the essence of this luminous house, designed by architect Robert Lund. In deference to the spectacular views, he replaced all extraneous walls with windows that look out from the living room (*above*) on the vivid blues of Moriches Bay. In turn, interior designer T. Keller Donovan picked up those blues and replayed them on stripes and borders in the sitting room (*opposite*), against a background of sand- and sisal-toned neutrals.

Designer Charlotte Moss, who creates both furniture and plans for interiors, worked on the exterior of her East Hampton home with the team of landscape architect Lisa Stamm and her architect husband-partner Dale Booher. Their joyous plantings around the pool and up the allée to the shingled Post-Modern house (*above*) include *Thalictrum Rochebrunianum* and urns overflowing with annuals, nierembergia, heliotrope, and *Anisodontea.* Booher's detail drawings of garden architecture hang behind horticultural works in progress in the potting shed (*opposite*).

Bright with the light from a classic arched window, the high, wide, and handsome sitting room of the house (*opposite*) has an almost alfresco feeling that is encouraged by sisal carpeting and generous helpings of flowers and plants. Reminiscent of Nancy Lancaster's approach to large spaces, Charlotte Moss's rich blend of antiques, patterns, and colors imparts a pleasant intimacy to the sitting area. To take full advantage of the room's soaring height, paintings and engravings are hung in layers high on the walls. By contrast, the dining area (*above*) is cozy, with painted chairs around a wicker table topped with a bouquet from the garden.

Spiked with hollyhocks that rise like fireworks over the herbaceous border, an English country-style garden (*opposite*) brightens the path to a vintage East Hampton carriage house (*above*). It was saved when the owners razed an old house and asked architect Jaquelin Taylor Robertson to design the new one (*top*), which may give a nod to the traditional Shingle style but is hardly a replay. Freed entirely from traditional foundation plantings, the house seems to float serenely on its vast expanse of lawn.

Wrapped with windows and detailed with linear woodwork, the sitting room of the house (*opposite, bottom*) takes its fresh attitude from monotone colors, leavened liberally with white. Interior designer Victoria Boris has repeated the architectural detailing for the glass-topped table. The photographs come from the owner's collection. Another collection, of rustic chairs, adds a folk touch to a hallway (*above*), where a nineteenth-century American hooked rug backs a quilt-covered table. Around the bedroom wall (*opposite, top*), a bit of poetic license: the last lines from Emerson's poem "Thine Eyes Still Shine."

NOTES

1. James Truslow Adams, *History of the Town of Southampton (East of Canoe Place)* (Bridgehampton, N.Y.: Hampton Press, 1918), 46.

2. Jason Epstein and Elizabeth Barlow, *East Hampton, A History and Guide* (New York: Random House, 1985), 16.

3. Ralph G. Duvall, *The History of Shelter Island, 1652–1932* (New York: Shelter Island Press, 1952), 30.

4. Horsford, Cornelia, "The Manor of Shelter Island," an address read before the annual meeting of The Order of Colonial Lords of Manors in America on April 23, 1931 (New York: printed privately, 1934).

5. Walter T. Punch, ed., *Keeping Eden: A History of Gardening in America* (Boston: Bulfinch Press, 1992), 10.

6. Katharine Cameron, *East Hampton: The 19th Century Artists' Paradise* (East Hampton, N.Y.: Guild Hall Museum, 1991), 2.

7. Elizabeth W. Champney, "The Summer Haunts of American Artists," *Century Magazine,* October 1885, quoted in Cameron, 5.

8. Charles De Kay, "A Happy Hunting Ground for Artists," *New York Times Illustrated Magazine,* May 14, 1899, 8–9, quoted in Ronald G. Pisano, *Long Island Landscape Painting 1820–1920* (Boston: New York Graphic Society, 1985), 9.

9. Cameron, 5.

10. Ibid.

BIBLIOGRAPHY

Abercrombie, Stanley. "Gwathmey Siegel." Monographs on Contemporary Architecture. Whitney Library of Design. New York: Watson-Guptill Publications, 1981.

Adams, James Truslow. *History of the Town of Southampton (East of Canoe Place).* Bridgehampton, N.Y.: Hampton Press, 1918.

Atkinson, D. Scott, and Nicolai Cikovsky, Jr. *William Merritt Chase: Summers at Shinnecock 1891–1962.* Washington: National Gallery of Art, 1987.

Braff, Phyllis. *Artists and East Hampton.* East Hampton, N.Y.: Guild Hall Museum, 1976.

————. *Thomas Moran.* East Hampton, N.Y.: Guild Hall Museum, 1980.

Broderick, Mosette Glaser. "A Place Where Nobody Goes. The Early Work of McKim Mead & White and the Development of the South Shore of Long Island." In *Search of Modern Architecture: A Tribute to Henry Russell Hitchcock,* edited by Helen Searling. The Architectural History Foundation, New York. Cambridge, Mass.: M.I.T. Press, 1982.

Cameron, Katharine. *East Hampton: The 19th Century Artists' Paradise.* East Hampton, N.Y.: Guild Hall Museum, 1991.

Close, Leslie Rose. *Portrait of an Era in Landscape Architecture. The Photographs of Mattie Edwards Hewitt.* Bronx, N.Y.: Wave Hill, 1983.

Dean, Ruth. *The Livable House; Its Garden.* New York: Moffat Yard & Co., 1917.

Doty, Robert, ed. *Jane Freilicher Paintings.* The Currier Gallery of Art. New York: Taplinger Publishing Co., 1986.

Duvall, Ralph G. *The History of Shelter Island, 1652–1932.* Shelter Island, N.Y., 1952. Supplement by Jean L. Schladermundt, 1932–1952.

Earle, Alice Morese. *Old Time Gardens.* New York: The Macmillan Company, 1901.

Eberlein, Harold Donilson. *Manor Houses and Historic Homes of Long Island and Staten Island.* New York: J. B. Lippincott, Co., 1928.

Epstein, Jason, and Elizabeth Barlow. *East Hampton, A History and Guide.* New York: Random House, 1985.

Fryxell, Fritof, ed. *Thomas Moran: Explorer in Search of Beauty.* East Hampton, N.Y.: Free Library, 1958.

Greene, Elaine. "Exit from the Fast Lane." *House Beautiful,* January 1991.

Griswold, Mac, and Eleanor Weller. *Golden Age of American Gardens: Proud Owners, Private Estates.* New York: Harry N. Abrams, 1991.

Halsey, Abigail Fithian. *In Old Southampton.* New York: Columbia University Press, 1940.

Halsey, Carolyn D. *The Revolution on Long Island.* New York: published privately, 1988.

Harrison, Helen A. *East Hampton Avant-Garde, A Salute to the Signa Gallery.* East Hampton, N.Y.: Guild Hall Museum, 1990.

Hefner, Robert J., ed. *East Hampton's Heritage: An Illustrated Architectural Record.* New York: W. W. Norton & Company, 1982.

————. *Windmills of Long Island.* Society of Preservation of Long Island Antiquities. New York: W. W. Norton & Co., 1983.

Hemphill, Christopher. "Hampton in the Hamptons." *Vanity Fair,* May 1985.

Horsford, Cornelia. "The Manor of Shelter Island." New York: printed privately, 1934.

Justin, Valerie. "The Brick Rugs of Margaret Kerr." *Oriental Rug Review,* June/July 1992.

Kimmelman, Michael. "Putting the Spotlight on Fairfield Porter." *New York Times,* October 9, 1992.

Lacy, Allen. "A New Influence in Gardens." *New York Times Magazine,* October 16, 1988.

Lamb, Martha. "The Manor of Shelter Island." *Magazine of American History,* November 1887.

Lawford, Valentine. "Gardens: Variety in Miniature." *Architectural Digest,* January 1979.

Leigh, Candace. "Margaret Kerr." *Dan's Papers,* September 15, 1989.

Leighton, Ann. *Early American Gardens.* Amherst: University of Massachusetts Press, 1986.

The Long Island Country House 1870–1930. The Parrish Art Museum. Los Angeles: Perpetua Press, 1988.

Lubow, Arthur. "The Creeks Revisited." *Vanity Fair,* August 1992.

Maass, John. *The Gingerbread Age. A View of Victorian America.* New York: Rinehart, 1957.

Murphy, Honoria, with Richard N. Billings. *Sara & Gerald: Villa America and After.* Alexandria, Va.: Times Books, 1982.

Murphy, Robert Cushman. "Fish-Shape Paumanok: Nature and Man on Long Island." Penrose Memorial Lecture for 1962. The American Philosophical Society, Philadelphia, 1962.

Pierson, George Wilson. *The Bringing of the Mill.* New Haven, Conn.: privately printed, n.d.

Pine, Robert H. *Sag Harbor. Past, Present and Future.* Sag Harbor, N.Y.: Sag Harbor Historic Preservation Commission, 1973.

Pisano, Ronald G. *A Leading Spirit in American Art: William Merritt Chase 1849–1916.* Seattle: Henry Art Gallery, University of Washington, 1983.

Pisano, Ronald G. *Long Island Landscape Painting 1820–1920.* Boston: New York Graphic Society, 1988.

Pisano, Ronald G. *Long Island Landscape Painting, Vol. II, The Twentieth Century.* Boston: Bulfinch Press, 1990.

Pisano, Ronald G. *Summer Afternoons / Landscape Paintings of William Merritt Chase.* Boston: Bulfinch Press, 1993.

Poole, Mary Jane, ed. *House & Garden's 26 Easy Little Gardens.* New York: Viking Press, 1975.

Popper, Ellen K. "Hamptons Houses Reverting to Traditional Style." *New York Times,* June 23, 1991.

Punch, Walter T., gen. ed. *Keeping Eden: A History of Gardening in America.* Massachusetts Horticultural Society. Boston: Bulfinch Press, 1992.

Rattray, Everett. *The South Fork.* Wainscott, N.Y.: Pushcart Publishing, 1979.

Rattray, Jeanette Edwards. *Up and Down Main Street.* East Hampton, N.Y.: *East Hampton Star,* 1968.

Rose, Barbara. *Krasner / Pollock. A Working Relationship.* East Hampton, N.Y.: Guild Hall Museum, 1981.

Samuels, Ellen. "The Guilded Age of Formal Gardens." *East Hampton Star,* March 31, 1988.

Sansone, Barbara. "Mr. Madoo." *Hamptons,* August 25, 1989.

Seager, Robert II. *And Tyler Too. A Biography of John & Julia Gardiner Tyler.* New York: McGraw-Hill Book Company, 1963.

Shelton, Louise. *Beautiful Gardens in America.* New York: Charles Scribner's Sons, 1915 (revised 1928).

Weisburg, Henry, and Lisa Donneson. *Guide to Sag Harbor.* Sag Harbor, N.Y.: John Street Press, 1975.

Wilson, Thurman. *Thomas Moran. Artist of the Mountain.* Norman: University of Oklahoma Press, 1966.

Ice-skating on Town Pond, East Hampton.

INDEX

PHOTO CREDITS:
Ed Watkins: half-title page; Bruce C. Jones: 5;
Noel Rowe: 31; Plakee/Jacobs: 35; Noel Rowe: 38;
Henderson Photography: 55; Noel Rowe: 67;
Noel Rowe: 87; Noel Rowe: 97; Bruce C. Jones: 99;
Noel Rowe: 109; Noel Rowe: 165; Plakee/Jacobs: 204.